MINISTER'S SERVICE MANUAL

BY

SAMUEL WARD HUTTON

"I can do all things in Him who strengthens me."
— Philippians 4:13.

"Do your best to present yourself to God as one approved, a workman who has no need to be ashamed."
— II Timothy 2:15a.

BAKER BOOK HOUSE
Grand Rapids, Michigan

PHOTOLITHOPRINTED BY CUSHING - MALLOY, INC.
ANN ARBOR, MICHIGAN, UNITED STATES OF AMERICA

PREFACE

Among ministers of non-liturgical churches there is increasing need for suitable forms, services, suggestions, guides, that the demands of today may be adequately and helpfully met. Ministering to the entire church constituency requires of the church staff a wealth of resource materials, that all things may be done with dignity and in good order.

In the ministry of today the original intent of the Master needs to be constantly kept in mind. At the same time there is constant need for adjustment in organization, method, staff, program of work, to match the demands of the present generation that the church may offer a complete ministry to all age groups from the cradle to the golden years.

To strengthen ministerial and lay leadership in an honest attempt to fulfill the pressing demands of their calling more completely, this *Service Manual* has been prepared as a guide to effective procedures. It is not aimed as a crutch, but rather is intended to stimulate initiative in thought and in appropriate action with the current opportunity and challenge in the foreground.

It is the sincere desire of the compiler to keep services free from cold, excessive formality; at the same time hold tenaciously to the spirit of freedom in providing reasonable moulds for ritual, symmetry in service design, dignity in content, and richness in worship values. Every occasion whether routine or special calls for full preparation and detailed handling.

The tendency of today is toward a synthesis of good form, spirit-filled, accurately-executed offices to the end that good taste may prevail. May this *Service Manual* serve well this purpose.

S. W. HUTTON

ACKNOWLEDGMENTS

Comrades among professional and lay leaders have been very generous in permitting the use of materials they have created. For this courtesy a word of grateful acknowledgment is given. Contributions toward the content of this *Manual* have been gathered through the years and where the source is known due recognition is given. If there is any error or oversight in giving credit abject apology is hereby offered.

The compiler is particularly indebted to Dr. Elmer D. Henson, Dr. Granville T. Walker, Dr. Dudley Strain, Dr. D. Ray Lindley, Dr. Noel L. Keith, Rev. Chester Crow, Rev. Thurman Morgan, Rev. G. N. Goldston, Rev. Frank C. Mabee, Jr., Rev. H. Daniel Morgan, Dr. Don J. VerDuin, Mrs. Pauline Thames, Reverend Jimmy Suggs, Miss Golda Wilhite and Mrs. George P. Fowler for valuable suggestions and criticisms.

Dr. D. Gordon Wiley, the Hennepin Avenue Methodist Church, Minneapolis, Minn., National Selected Morticians, Evanston, Ill., National Council of Churches of Christ in the United States of America, Rev. Sidney Hawkins, Rev. Benjamin L. Smith, The Secret Place, The Bethany Press, Dr. Peter Ainslie, Dr. H. C. Armstrong, Mrs. Bessie Hart, Mrs. Jay D. Howell, Rev. Claude E. Stinson, and numerous other leaders in many religious bodies have shared in the material presented in this volume.

For the use of poems and other items included in this volume the writer is deeply indebted. It is the sincere desire of all, whose heart interests are expressed in program, poem, prose and other materials, that by making these items, in organized setting, available through this book, a lasting and helpful contribution will have been made to the Christian ministry in its various needs.

S. W. HUTTON

A MINISTER'S DEDICATION

To this day that is mine, my country's and my God's I dedicate my all. My talents, every one, shall be held subject to the sight draft of the emergencies of others. I will enlarge my soul by cultivating love for those from whom I find myself recoiling. No man shall ever feel his color or his caste in my presence, for within my heart of hearts there shall be no consciousness of it.

The man who has fallen shall find me a friend, the woman down, a helper. But more than this, those falling shall have my trust that they may stand again. The cry of every child shall find my heart whether cry of need or of aspiration. Not one of all the nation's "little ones" shall be despised. Cherishing every life of whatever land or race and mindful of hidden struggles in all things I will strive to help and to serve.

No word shall ever pass my lips that hurts another in things of face, form, station, or estate. My own weaknesses, my foibles and my sins shall chasten speech and deny my pride. My life shall be a dedicated thing. I shall count it desecration to pervert it. The vandal hands of lust and hate and greed shall not be permitted to despoil.

And thus I resolve, not because I am good, but that I want to be; not because I am strong, but that I feel weakness; not that I feel above others, but with all my soul I long to be of humankind, both helped and helper. So do I dedicate my days. So do I set apart my culture. So do I receive but give to others. So do I press humbly into the presence of the sacrificial Son of Man, crying out in eager consecration, "Let me follow Thee, Master," wherever the world still needs ministry, wherever life is still to be given for many.

Help me, Thou whose manger cradle brought democracy to light, to meet in my own worth democracy's final test and to my own great day be true.

Charles S. Medbury

CONTENTS

CHAPTER I

THE MINISTER AND THE MARRIAGE RITE

PRE-MARRIAGE COUNSELING

This Manual, while designed primarily for the minister, may be quite serviceable to others as well. The marriage rite includes many people and requires major decisions. It is exceedingly important that the church plan for youth such a wholesome atmosphere and such a complete program to match the needs of youth that in the matter of dating, "going steady," the engagement, and the marriage the minister and the church may have the respect and the confidence of the young people.

It is quite appropriate for the minister to serve as consultant, that he (and his wife) may guide the interested parties to the marriage relationship past the pitfalls of commercialism and ostentation, through the normal channel of a beautiful religious rite ordained of God in His master-plan for the ongoing of the race. Youth leaders in the local church can work with the minister in this procedure.

Fortunately there is a wealth of timely literature available for guidance all along the marriage pathway. Initial plans, major decisions, the when, where, formal or informal, how much is to be spent, who is to be invited—all of these and many other matters are considered. These helps are available. Following the trail toward marriage a schedule of preparation is vital, the wardrobe, the rehearsal, the processional, the ceremony, the recessional, the reception, the wedding trip, establishing a home, a home dedication service sponsored by the church, furnishings for the home, also problems attending married life. In all of these matters, and even through premarital guidance of a more intimate nature, the church through the minister may give help to young people at a time when it is very natural and most needed. This is the high tide. Use it to lift individuals, ideals, institutions.

THE LAW

Before a minister solemnizes a marriage he should acquaint himself with the laws of the state in which the marriage is to be performed. The office of the county clerk will be in position to furnish all information needed.

In some states it is required that the minister be registered and have a state license, the number of which must be recorded on every marriage certificate. In a large number of states a license must be issued to each couple before marriage. The laws vary in different states.

If a minister performs a marriage ceremony without legal warrant the marriage is valid, but the minister is subject to fine and even imprisonment.

The essential element of every marriage ceremony is the mutual agreement of the contracting parties before witnesses that they take each other as husband and wife. Any form is valid which provides for this mutual agreement. Most states require that there be witnesses.

Around these fundamental considerations we have arranged the marriage ceremonies and customs. In the interest of good order, and to invest so important a contract with appropriate and religious significance, due regard to dignified and religious ceremonials should be given at all times.

Society has a right to know the contracting parties are to be recognized as living together as husband and wife. A record of all marriages should be kept by the minister. The thoughtful minister will keep a record of his own; a copy of this record will be sent to the authority issuing the license, and, a certificate will be given to the contracting parties.

THE CEREMONY

(1) The Marriage Pageant

There is great variety of taste in regard to the marriage ceremony and its accompanying pageantry. The bride stands on the left of the groom during the ceremony; the bridesmaids stand on the left of the bride; the best man and the groomsmen on the right of the groom. If the father of the bride gives the bride away he should stand to the right of the minister and a little to the rear, then after giving the bride away take his seat beside the bride's mother.

The order of the bridal procession is not the special responsibility of the minister, but he is frequently consulted and a request for guidance should be promptly met by him. A professional consultant is often available. (A further word on this matter will be found on page 20 of this *Manual*.)

Young ministers may find the following diagram helpful. It is offered as a typical arrangement, and may be adapted to the local situation. The bride and her mother should be given freedom of choice in these matters.

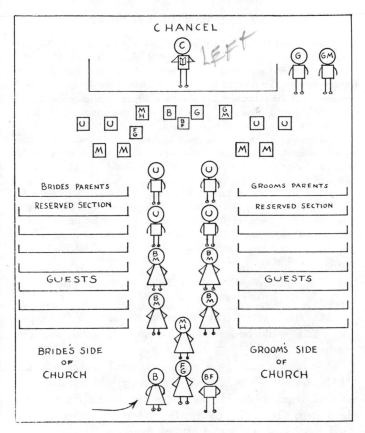

THE PROCESSION

The wedding procession may vary. This diagram suggests four ushers and four bridesmaids, two of each on either side. Note the figures as they enter, then the station for each person.

Meaning of symbols: B - Bride, G - Groom, MH - Maid (or Matron) of Honor, C-Clergyman, GM-Groomsman, BF-Bride's Father, U - Usher, FG - Flower-girl. A ring-bearer may be included if desired.

It is understood that the Clergyman, the Groom and the Grooms-man will enter from the right side of the chancel when possible. Others will enter from the rear.

(2) The Marriage Ceremony

History and tradition have provided for the minister reliable marriage etiquette upon which he may depend, also there are always available well-defined ceremonies, some very elaborate and formal, others quite simple. The contracting couple will have something to say both in regard to the ceremony and the place where it is to be conducted.

Whether the ceremony is carried out in the minister's residence, in another home, in a wedding chapel, or in a church sanctuary—in reasonable simplicity or with great elaboration—the minister should always examine the license ahead of time to see that it is in regular form and that he is authorized as a minister of the Gospel to perform the ceremony.

Eventually every minister will develop a ceremony essentially his own, probably a very simple one, and, in addition one that is more elaborate. The Book of Common Prayer as Used by the Protestant Episcopal Church in the United States is one of the usual sources for stately, elaborate form. Here is one the compiler of this *Manual* has used to good advantage—

> The persons to be married having taken their places
> before the minister, he shall say:

℟ MARRIAGE is a sacred institution, the basis of human society, and should be held in high honor among all men and women.

We are assembled here in the presence of God, to join this MAN and this WOMAN in holy marriage; which is instituted of God, regulated by His commandments, and blessed by our Lord Jesus Christ. Let us therefore reverently remember that God has established and sanctified marriage for the welfare and happiness of mankind.

Our Saviour has declared that a man shall leave his father and mother and cleave unto his wife. By His apostles, He has instructed those who enter into this relation to cherish a mutual esteem and love; to bear with each other's infirmities and weaknesses; to comfort each other in sickness, trouble and sorrow; in honesty and industry to provide for each other and for their household, in temporal things; to pray for and encourage

12

each other in things pertaining to God; and to live together as heirs of his grace.

Who gives this woman to be married?

(The father of the bride says, "I do," then retires to his seat.) *TAKE HAND*

For as much as these two persons have come to this house of worship (or home) to be made one in the holy relationship of marriage, it is understood that neither of them, nor others present, are aware of any just reason why the contracting parties may not be lawfully joined.

I charge you both, before our God and Father, the Searcher of all hearts, that if either of you know any reason why you may not lawfully be joined together in matrimony you do now make it known. For should any persons be joined together otherwise than in harmony with the will of God, their union is not blessed of Him. *I COR. 13*

(Let us pray.) *Kin HAS A PRAYER*

Our Father, whose presence brings happiness to every condition, and whose favor sweetens every relation in life; we pray Thee to be present and to favor these two persons that they may be truly joined in the honorable estate of marriage.

As they have been brought together by Thy providence, sanctify them by Thy Spirit, and grant them full understanding of their new relationship. Enrich their lives by Thy grace, that they may enjoy the comforts, undergo the cares, endure the trials, and perform the duties of life together as Christian people under Thy guidance and protection; through our Saviour Jesus the Christ. Amen.

M.., do you solemnly agree before God and these witnesses to take this WOMAN to be your lawful, wedded wife; to love and respect her, honor and cherish her, in health and in sickness, in prosperity and in adversity; and,

13

leaving all others, to keep yourself only unto her, so long as you both shall live?

"I do."

W.................................., do you in like manner solemnly agree to receive this MAN as your lawful, wedded husband; to love and respect him; and to live with him in all faith and tenderness, in health and in sickness, in prosperity and in adversity; and leaving all others to keep yourself only unto him, so long as you both shall live?

"I do."

(Will you please join hands and repeat the following lines after me:)

I,.................................., take you, ..., to be my wedded wife; and I do promise and covenant, before God and these witnesses, to be your loving and faithful husband, in plenty and in want, in joy and in sorrow, in sickness and in health, as long as we both shall live.

(She repeats the following:)

I,.................................., take you, ..., to be my wedded husband, and I do promise and covenant, before God and these witnesses, to be your loving and faithful wife, in plenty and in want, in joy and in sorrow, in sickness and in health, as long as we both shall live.

(I believe you have a ring.)

May this beautiful token and pledge symbolize the purity and endlessness of your love.

(The groom places the ring on the fourth finger of the bride's left hand and repeats after the minister)

This ring I give to you, in token and pledge, of our constant faith, and abiding love.

14

(If the bride has a ring for the groom the same
words may be repeated.)

(Let us pray.)

Heavenly Father, we have heard from these two persons
the acceptance of the solemn and significant vows of marriage.
Do Thou grant unto them grace and courage, love and loyalty,
constancy and faith to maintain these vows to the end of
the way.

May this new home radiate the sunshine of Thy love, and
may every heart that comes in contact with this home in its
several relationships be enriched and ennobled.

Through Christ our Lord who shares in this sacred institution. Amen.

By the authority committed unto me as a Minister of the
Gospel, I declare .... and ....
are now Husband and Wife, according to the ordinance of
God and the law of the state.

God having joined these together in Marriage, let no man
seek to dissolve this union.

(May we look to the Father of us all for His blessing and benediction.)

"The Lord bless you and keep you;
    The Lord make his face to shine upon you,
        and be gracious unto you;
    The Lord lift up his countenance upon you,
        and give you peace."
In the name of our sinless Master, even Jesus
    the Christ. Amen. —Numbers 6:24-26.

15

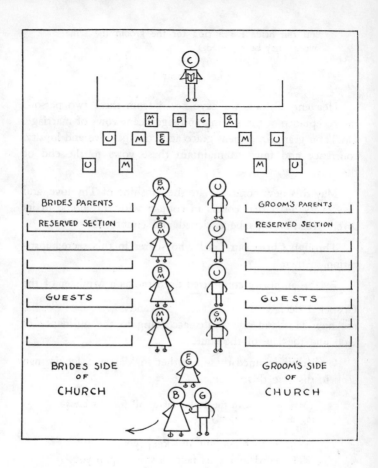

THE RECESSION

Moving from their stations the wedding recession leaves as indicated, the bride and groom leading the way. The bridesmaids may walk side by side, followed by ushers, or walk with ushers. The groomsman will walk with the maid, or matron, of honor. The flower-girl walks immediately behind the bride and groom.

RECEIVING LINE AT RECEPTION

Immediately inside the entrance of the room in which the reception is held: 1. Mother of the Bride, 2. Father of the Groom, 3. Mother of the Groom, 4. Father of the Bride, 5, 6. Bridesmaids, 7. Honor Attendant (Maid or Matron of Honor), 8. Bride, 9. Groom (the bride is on the right of the Groom), 10, 11. Bridesmaids. The Groomsman and Ushers are not in the line.

A BRIEF SCRIPTURAL MARRIAGE CEREMONY
(This form may be used in a home, or in a church
where a short service is requested.)

FRIENDS, we are assembled in the sight of God and in the presence of these witnesses to join together this man and this woman in Holy Matrimony; which is an honorable estate, instituted of God, and adorned by our Lord Jesus Christ by his presence and the first miracle that he wrought in Cana of Galilee. It is commended by the Apostle Paul to be honorable among all men; and therefore is not to be entered into lightly, but reverently, soberly, discretely.

The Holy Scriptures set before you the love of Christ for His Church as an example for your devotion. You are not left without guidance concerning the meaning of that love. These are the words of the Great Apostle:

"Love is patient and kind; love is not jealous or boastful; it is not arrogant or rude. Love does not insist on its own way; it is not irritable or resentful; it does not rejoice at wrong, but rejoices in the right. Love bears all things, believes all things, hopes all things, endures all things. Love never ends."

—I Cor. 13 (in part).

Into such a union you come now to be joined. If either of you, or if anyone present knows any just cause why this marriage should not be solemnized, I charge you to make it known at this time or hereafter to remain silent.

17

(Then shall the minister say:)

Do you, _____. take this woman to be your lawful, wedded wife, to love and to cherish, to have and to hold, and forsaking all others to keep yourself to her only so long as you both shall live?

(The bridegroom replies:)

"I do."

(Then shall the minister say:)

Do you, _____, take this man to be your lawful, wedded husband, to love and to cherish, to have and to hold, and forsaking all others to keep yourself to him only so long as you both shall live?

(The bride replies)

"I do."

Have you a ring?

(The groom shall place the ring on the fourth finger
of the bride's left hand and repeat after the minister:)

This ring I give thee in token and pledge of our constant faith and abiding love.

(If the bride gives a ring follow the same procedure.
Then the minister shall say—)

Inasmuch as you have agreed together to enter the holy rite of wedlock, and have given and received a ring in token and in pledge of your love, I now declare you husband and wife in the name of Christ our Lord and Master.

(Then the minister shall pray:)

The Lord God Almighty, bless, preserve and keep you. The Lord with His favor mercifully look upon you and fill you with all spiritual grace, that you may so live together in this life that in the world to come you may have life everlasting, through Jesus Christ, our Lord. Amen.

THE CERTIFICATE OF MARRIAGE

Marriage certificates may be purchased in many forms and for a wide range of prices. It is wise for a minister to keep a supply on hand, and to issue a certificate immediately after the wedding, or at least within a few days. If there is need for a form the following is offered for consideration:

THIS IS TO CERTIFY that, in accordance with the Laws of God and

of the State of_____

Mr. _____ of _____

and

M _____ of _____
were by me, a minister of the Gospel, united in Holy Matrimony, at

_____, in the County of_____,

and State of_____, on the_____

of_____in the year of our Lord 19_____

The marriage above was performed by virtue of a License duly

issued by the Clerk of the Court of_____County

and of the State above named, the said License Number_____

bearing date_____19_____

_____

_____

Minister's Signature and Address

_____

_____

_____

Witnesses

Chapter II

THE MINISTER SERVES IN TIME OF ILLNESS, TROUBLE OR SORROW

In the Home

At the Hospital

In the Last Hours

In a Memorial, or Funeral Service

In Using Appropriate Scriptural Selections

Through Suitable Hymns and Poems

In Planning Appropriate Messages

A large portion of the minister's work will be with those who are in trouble. Bruised and broken hearts need the ministry of one who understands. Trouble stalks the pathway of life disguised in many forms.

Sometimes disappointment or serious illness shatters the hopes of a household. Financial reverses mar the tranquility of a well-ordered family. A wayward son, an erring daughter, a reckless brother bring sadness, disgrace and heartbreak to a home. A tragic accident or untimely death smashes ruthlessly into another home. Hearts are aching and need the ministry of comfort and understanding.

Into such tragic hours as these the minister is privileged to come with a ministry of kindness, understanding, helpfulness.

Do not hesitate, go immediately, comfort your people and as you grasp their hands in helpfulness they will slip into your keeping the key to their hearts.

Perhaps you may help to right a wrong. Those you serve will love you ever afterward. A frank talk with those involved may halt misunderstanding, or heal a festering sore spot. By honest, loving dealing you may save further tragedy. Nathan did a full day's work when he dealt frankly with David, "Thou art the man."

If a son or daughter has fallen into open disgrace go at once to the home. You as an elder brother may be able to give wise and confidential counsel. This is no time to condemn, but rather to show an understanding spirit.

If tidings of serious sickness come, lose no time in visiting that home; a soul may be near eternity and want your prayers. If a business man has met with crushing reverses, go to him; give him a warm hand shake, a word of understanding. He will never forget it. The hand-hold to eternal things is on your side.

Do not try to stop the tears of those in real sorrow, or deep grief. Tears relieve sorrowing hearts and often keep them from breaking. Gradually, gently, lead the sorrowing to think of the other side. True comfort comes when we think things through in the light of the eternal purposes of God for each of us. An appropriate prayer, placed quite naturally at the proper moment will help mightily.

If it seems wise to read the Scriptures in the home where trouble has come, read briefly, then pray in the spirit of consolation with direct reference to those in trouble. Use whole portions of Scripture where possible rather than scattered verses. Preface each Scripture with a brief introductory word of background.

SCRIPTURES FOR THE TROUBLED

Psalm 46 (See page 40)

You will say in that day: "I will give thanks to thee, O Lord, for though thou wast angry with me, thy anger turned away, and thou didst comfort me. Behold God is my salvation; I will trust, and will not be afraid; for the Lord God is my strength and my song, and he has become my salvation."—Isaiah 12:1, 2.

". . . Thou dost keep him in perfect peace, whose mind is stayed on thee, because he trusts in thee. Trust in the Lord forever, for the Lord God is an everlasting rock. For he has brought low the inhabitants of the height, the lofty city. He lays it low, lays it low to the ground, casts it to the dust, the foot tramples it, the feet of the poor, the steps of the needy." The way of the righteous is level; thou dost make smooth the path of the righteous. In the paths of thy judgments, O Lord, we wait for thee; thy memorial name is the desire of our soul. My soul yearns for thee in the night, my spirit within me earnestly seeks thee, for when thy judgments are in the earth, the inhabitants of the world learn righteousness.—Isaiah 26:3-9.

Let not your hearts be troubled; believe in God, believe also in me. In my Father's house are many rooms; if it were not so, would I have told you that I go to prepare a place for you? And when I go and prepare a place for you, I will come again and will take you to myself, that where I am you may be also. And you know the way where I am going. Thomas said to him, "Lord, we do not know where you are going; how can we know the way?" Jesus said to him, "I am the way, and the truth, and the life, no one comes to the Father, but by me. If you had known me, you would have known my Father also, henceforth you know him and have seen him." "Peace I leave with you; my peace I give to you. Not as the world gives do I give to you. Let not your hearts be troubled, neither let them be afraid."—John 14:1-7, 27.

We know that in everything God works for good with those who love him, who are called according to his purpose. What then shall we say to this? If God is for us, who is against us? No, in all things we are more than conquerors through him who loved us. For I am sure that neither death, nor life, nor angels, nor principalities, nor things present nor things to come, nor powers, nor height, nor depth, nor anything else in all creation, will be able to separate us from the love of God in Christ Jesus our Lord.—Romans 8:28, 31, 37-39.

Cast all your anxieties on him, for he cares about you. Be sober, be watchful. Your adversary, the devil prowls around like a roaring lion, seeking someone to devour. Resist him, firm in your faith, knowing that the same experience of suffering is required of your brotherhood throughout the world. And after you have suffered a little while, the God of all grace, who has called you to his eternal glory in Christ, will himself restore, establish, and strengthen you. To him be the dominion for ever and ever. Amen.—I Peter 5:7-11.

SCRIPTURES FOR USE IN TIME OF SICKNESS

The Lord is my shepherd, I shall not want; he makes me lie down in green pastures. He leads me beside still waters; he restores my soul. He leads me in paths of righteousness for his name's sake. Even though I walk through the valley of the shadow of death, I fear no evil; for thou art with me; thy rod and thy staff they comfort me. Thou preparest a table before me in the presence of my enemies; thou anointest my head with oil, my cup overflows. Surely goodness and mercy shall follow me all the days of my life; and I shall dwell in the house of the Lord forever.—Psalm 23.

The Lord is my light and my salvation; whom shall I fear? The Lord is the stronghold of my life; of whom shall I be afraid? When evildoers assail me, uttering slanders against me, my adversaries and foes, they shall stumble and fall. Though a host encamp against me, my heart shall not fear; though war arise against me, yet I will be confident. One thing have I asked of the Lord, that will I seek after; that I may dwell in the house of the Lord all the days of my life, to behold the beauty of the Lord, and to inquire in his temple. For he will hide me in his shelter in the day of trouble; he will conceal me under the cover of his tent, he will set me high upon a rock. And now my head shall be lifted up above my enemies round about me; and I will offer in his tent sacrifices with shouts of joy; I will sing and make melody to the Lord.— Psalm 27:1-6.

Be still, and know that I am God. I am exalted among the nations, I am exalted in the earth! The Lord of hosts is with us; the God of Jacob is our refuge.—Psalm 46:10, 11.

Praise the Lord. I will give thanks to the Lord with my whole heart, in the company of the upright, in the congregation. Great are the works of the Lord, studied by all who have pleasure in them. Full of honor and majesty is his work, and his righteousness endures for ever. He has caused his wonderful works to be remembered; the Lord is gracious and merciful. He provides food for those who fear him; he is ever mindful of his covenant. He has shown his people the power of his works, in giving them the heritage of the nations. The works of his hands are faithful and just; all his precepts are trustworthy, they are established for ever and ever, to be performed with faithfulness and uprightness. He sent redemption to his people; he has commanded his covenant for ever. Holy and terrible is his name! The fear of the Lord is the beginning of wisdom; a good understanding have all those who practice it. His praise endures forever!—Psalm 111.

I will lift up my eyes to the hills. From whence does my help come? My help comes from the Lord, who made heaven and earth. He will not let your foot be moved, he who keeps you will not slumber. Behold, he who keeps Israel will neither slumber nor sleep. The Lord is your keeper; the Lord is your shade on your right hand. The sun shall not smite you by day, nor the moon by night. The Lord will keep you from all evil; he will keep your life. The Lord will keep your going out and your coming in from this time forth and forevermore.—Psalm 121.

A voice cries: "In the wilderness prepare the way of the Lord, make straight in the desert a highway for our God. Every valley shall be lifted up, and every mountain and hill be made low; the uneven ground shall become level, and the rough places a plain. And the glory of the Lord shall be revealed, and all flesh shall see it together, for the mouth of the Lord has spoken." He will feed his flock like a shepherd, he will gather the lambs in his arms, he will carry them in his bosom, and gently lead those that are with young. He gives power to the faint, and to him who has no might he increases strength. Even youths shall faint and be weary, and young men shall fall exhausted; but they who wait for the Lord shall renew their strength, they shall mount up with wings like eagles, they shall run and not be weary, they shall walk and not faint.—Isaiah 40:3-5, 11, 29-31.

". . . I am the good shepherd. The good shepherd lays down his life for the sheep. He who is a hireling and not a shepherd, whose own the sheep are not, sees the wolf coming and leaves the sheep and flees; and the wolf snatches them and scatters them. He flees because he is a hireling and cares nothing for the sheep. I am the good shepherd; I know my own and my own know me, as the Father knows me and I know the Father; and I lay down my life for the sheep. And I have other sheep, that are not of this fold; I must bring them also, and they will heed my voice. So there shall be one flock, one shepherd. For this reason the Father loves me, because I lay down my life, that I may take it again. No one takes it from me, but I lay it down of my own accord. I have power to lay it down

26

and I have power to take it again; this charge I have received from my Father."—John 10:11-18.

And I saw the holy city, new Jerusalem, coming down out of heaven from God, prepared as a bride adorned for her husband; and I heard a great voice from the throne saying, "Behold, the dwelling of God is with men. He will dwell with them, and they shall be his people, and God himself will be with them; he will wipe away every tear from their eyes, and death shall be no more, neither shall there be mourning nor crying nor pain any more, for the former things have passed away."—Revelation 21:2-4.

IN THE HOSPITAL
A Ministry to Those in a Hospital, a Rest Home, or Other Institution of Healing and Comfort

We are exceedingly fortunate to live in a land where surgery, medical attention, nursing care and other appropriate ministries are made available. In ministering to those who are confined to these institutions the Scriptures offered in the preceding and following paragraphs may be used. It may well be made clear to the patient you are visiting that in all this array of medical science we are seeking to work with God, in whose image we are created, in restoring normal physical and mental well-being.

A brief prayer of confidence, faith and understanding with one who is to undergo surgery is exceedingly helpful. A prayer of gratitude after successful surgery is worthy procedure. In times like these the hearts of men are open wide for spiritual sustenance.

The values of having a chapel in the hospital to which one may repair for comfort and spiritual strength may be suggested. To lend the spirit of cooperation with those in whose skills we share is helpful in itself. In these days when blood transfusions are very common we discover more definitely than ever that God has made us of one blood.

IN THE LAST HOURS
Scriptures for the Christian Whose Life Is Ebbing Away

Create in me a clean heart, O God, and put a new and right spirit within me. Cast me not away from thy presence, and take not thy holy Spirit from me. Restore to me the joy of thy salvation, and uphold me with a willing spirit. O Lord, open thou my lips, and my mouth shall show forth thy praise. —Psalm 51:10-12, 15.

Ho, every one who thirsts, come to the waters; and he who has no money, come buy and eat! Seek the Lord while he may be found, call upon him while he is near; let the wicked forsake his way, and the unrighteous man his thoughts; let him return to the Lord, that he may have mercy on him, and to our God, for he will abundantly pardon. For my thoughts are not your thoughts, neither are your ways my ways, says the Lord. For as the heavens are higher than the earth, so are my ways higher than your ways and my thoughts than your thoughts. For as the rain and the snow come down from heaven, and return not thither but water the earth, making it bring forth and sprout, giving seed to the sower and bread to the eater, so shall my word be that goes forth from my mouth; it shall not return to me empty, but it shall accomplish that which I purpose, and prosper in the thing for which I sent it. For you shall go out in joy, and be led forth in peace; the mountains and the hills before you shall break forth into singing, and all the trees of the field shall clap their hands. Instead of the thorn shall come up the cypress; instead of the brier shall come up the myrtle; and it shall be to the Lord for a memorial, for an everlasting sign which shall not be cut off. —Isaiah 55:1a, 6-13.

Come to me, all who labor, and are heavy-laden, and I will give you rest. Take my yoke upon you, and learn from me; for I am gentle and lowly in heart, and you will find rest for your souls. For my yoke is easy, and my burden is light.— Matthew 11:28-30.

Lord, now lettest thou thy servant depart in peace, according to they word; for mine eyes have seen thy salvation which thou hast prepared in the presence of all people, a light for revelation to the gentiles, and for glory to thy people Israel. —Luke 2:29-32.

For God so loved the world that he gave his only Son, that whoever believes in him should not perish but have eternal life. For God sent the Son into the world, not to condemn the world, but that the world might be saved through him. He who believes in him is not condemned; he who does not believe is condemned already, because he has not believed in the name of the only Son of God. And this is the judgment, that the light has come into the world, and men loved darkness rather than light, because their deeds were evil. For every one who does evil hates the light, and does not come to the light, lest his deeds should be exposed. But he who does what is true comes to the light, that it may be clearly seen that his deeds have been wrought in God.—John 3:16-21.

Jesus said to her, "I am the resurrection and the life; he who believes in me, though he die, yet shall he live, and whoever lives and believes in me shall never die. Do you believe this?" She said to him, "Yes, Lord; I believe that you are the Christ, the Son of God, he who is coming into the world." —John 11:25, 26.

Therefore, since we are surrounded by so great a cloud of witnesses, let us also lay aside every weight, and sin which clings so closely, and let us run with perseverance the race that is set before us, looking to Jesus the pioneer and perfecter of our faith, who for the joy that was set before him endured the cross, despising the shame, and is seated at the right hand of the throne of God.—Hebrews 12:1, 2.

IN THE HOUR OF DEATH
Scriptures for Use in the Home Where
Death Has Come

Be strong, and let your heart take courage, all you who wait for the Lord. O how abundant is thy goodness, which thou hast laid up for those who fear thee, and wrought for those who take refuge in thee. . . . In the covert of thy presence thou hidest them.—Psalm 31:24, 19, 20a.

The eternal God is your dwelling place, and underneath are the everlasting arms.—Deuteronomy 33:27.

I sought the Lord and he answered me, and delivered me from all my fears. Look to him and be radiant; so your faces shall never be ashamed. The angel of the Lord encamps around those who fear him, and delivers them. O taste and see that the Lord is good! Happy is the man who takes refuge in him. O fear the Lord, you his saints, for those who fear him have no want!—Psalm 34:4, 5, 7-9.

Bless the Lord, O my soul; and all that is within me bless his holy name! Bless the Lord, O my soul and forget not all his benefits, who forgives all your iniquity, who heals all your diseases, who redeems your life from the pit, who crowns you with steadfast love and mercy, who satisfies you with good as long as you live so that your youth is renewed like the eagle's. The Lord works vindication and justice for all who are oppressed. He made known his ways to Moses, his acts to the people of Israel. The Lord is mericiful and gracious, slow to anger and abounding in steadfast love. He will not always chide, nor will he keep his anger forever. He does not deal with us according to our sins, nor requite us according to our iniquities. For as the heavens are high above the earth, so great is his steadfast love toward those who fear him; as far as the east is from the west, so far does he remove our transgressions from us. As a father pities his children, so the Lord pities those who fear him. For he knows our frame; he remembers that we are dust. As for man, his days are like grass; he flourishes like a flower of the field; for the wind passes over it, and it is gone, and its place knows it no more, but the steadfast love of the Lord is from everlasting to everlasting upon those who fear him, and his righteousness to children's children, to those who keep his covenant and remember to do his commandments.—Psalm 103:1-18.

But we have this treasure in earthen vessels, to show that the transcendent power belongs to God and not to us. We are afflicted in every way, but not crushed; perplexed but not driven to despair; persecuted, but not forsaken; struck down but not destroyed; always carrying in the body the death of Jesus, so that the life of Jesus may also be manifested in our bodies. For while we live we are always being given up to death for Jesus' sake, so that the life of Jesus may be manifested in our mortal flesh. So death is at work in us, but life in you. So we do not lose heart. Though our outer nature is wasting away, our inner nature is being renewed every day. For this slight momentary affliction is preparing for us an eternal weight of glory beyond all comparison, because we look not to the things that are seen, but to the things that are unseen; for the things that are seen are transient, but the things that are unseen are eternal.—II Corinthians 4:7-12, 16-18.

Count it all joy, my brethren, when you meet various trials, for you know that the testing of your faith produces steadfastness. And let steadfastness have its full effect, that you may be perfect and complete, lacking in nothing. Blessed is the man who endures trial, for when he has stood the test he will receive the crown of life which God has promised to those who love him.—James 1:2-4, 12.

(Follow the reading of Scripture with a brief prayer.)

IN A MEMORIAL OR FUNERAL SERVICE
IMPORTANT SUGGESTIONS TO THE MINISTER

As soon as the minister knows that he is to have charge of the funeral service he should hasten to the home of the deceased to offer comfort to the bereaved. He should ascertain the wishes of the family concerning the funeral arrangements and carry out these wishes in a manner to give confidence, comfort and complete satisfaction. This service calls for good taste and tact. It is, in all probability, the time when the minister gets closest to his people—when the heart-strings are vibrant.

The simpler the burial service the better, but let this service be full of heart power and sincere sympathy. The minister does not speak as a judge in relation to the deceased, but rather as a comforter to the bereaved.

The minister, particularly the younger minister, will probably address more people in the funeral, or memorial service, than on any other occasion. He should therefore make ample, thoughtful preparation.

A brief obituary may be read to bring before the assembly of relatives and friends a few essential facts regarding the deceased. A brief story of the life of the deceased, spoken in high appreciation of the sterling qualities of character exemplified, will often be very appropriate. In any event the minister will do well to make ample preparation for a funeral service that he may say and do that which is right.

It is worthy practice for the minister to return with the family to the home of the deceased after the memorial service. Some of the most effective ministries of comfort and understanding can be offered at this time. The tension has been released, there is the satisfaction that all that is possible has been done to lay away the body of the loved one in reasonable dignity and order. The hearts of relatives are open for kindly suggestions from the minister. It will be possible for the minister to get acquainted with other members of the family and circle of friends. Lasting and helpful contacts will be possible.

FORMS FOR FUNERAL OR MEMORIAL SERVICES

The order of service for a funeral should be simple. Several factors must be taken into account. It is wise to honor requests of the family of the deceased wherever possible. A service held in a home, or mortuary, will usually be less formal and quite brief. Local practice is usually a sufficient guide.

While brevity and simplicity are usually followed, the service for a prominent citizen, in which several ministers participate, will require more time.

Usually this complete order may be followed:

> Music
> Opening Scriptural Sentences
> Invocation
> Hymn
> Scripture Lesson
> Pastoral Prayer
> Funeral Message
> Benediction

The following variation may serve as a suitable pattern:

> Instrumental Music (Hymns of Comfort)
> Scriptural Sentences
> Prayer of Invocation
> Hymn
> Scripture Selections
> Pastoral Prayer
> Hymn
> Obituary, or Life Story
> Memorial Address
> Hymn
> Benediction
> Instrumental Music

Still another variation may be used:

> Hymns of Comfort
> Scripture Reading
> Prayer
> Funeral Message
> Prayer

> (Service concluded at the grave with
> Scripture Reading
> Poem, or Committal
> Benediction)

For additional guidance in regard to conducting funerals please consult *A Living Hope.* Suggestions for Funeral Services arranged by Jesse Halsey, published by The Abingdon-Cokesbury Press, Nashville, Tennessee.

(The minister shall precede the casket to the grave, and after the casket has been placed, he will stand at the head thereof, and shall say:)

"We brought nothing into this world, and it is certain we can carry nothing out.'| The Lord gave, and the Lord has taken away; blessed be the name of the Lord.—Job 1:21. (The portion in quotation is a paraphrase of the first portion of Job 1:21.)

Lo! I tell you a mystery. We shall not all sleep, but we shall all be changed, in a moment, in the twinkling of an eye, at the last trumpet. For the trumpet will sound and the dead will be raised imperishable and we shall be changed. For this perishable nature must put on the imperishable, and this mortal nature must put on immortality. When the perishable puts on the imperishable, and the mortal puts on immortality, then shall come to pass the saying that is written:

"Death is swallowed up in victory."

"O death, where is thy victory?

O death, where is thy sting?"

The sting of death is sin, and the power of sin is the law. But thanks be to God, who gives us the victory through our Lord Jesus Christ.

Therefore, my beloved brethren, be steadfast, immovable, always abounding in the work of the Lord, knowing that in the Lord your labor is not in vain.—I Corinthians 15:51-58.

(Then shall the minister say:)

Forasmuch as the spirit of our deceased................................has returned to God who gave it, we therefore commit .... body to its kindred elements; looking for the general resurrection in the last day, and the life of the world to come, through our Lord Jesus Christ; at whose second coming in glorious majesty

to judge the world, the earth and the sea shall give up
dead; and the perishable bodies of those who sleep in
shall be changed, and made like unto his own glorious b
according to the mighty working whereby he is able to subdue
all things unto himself.

(Then shall the minister pronounce the benediction.)

Now may the God of peace who brought again from the
dead our Lord Jesus, the Great Shepherd of the sheep, by the
blood of the eternal covenant, equip you with everything good
that you may do his will, working in you that which is pleasing
in his sight, through Jesus Christ; to whom be glory for ever
and ever. Amen.—Hebrews 13:20.

II

(The minister standing at the head of the casket may say:)

But we would not have you ignorant, brethren, concerning
those who are asleep, that you may not grieve as others do
who have no hope. For since we believe that Jesus died and
rose again, even so, through Jesus, God will bring with him
those who have fallen asleep. For this we declare to you by
the word of the Lord, that we who are alive, who are left until
the coming of the Lord, shall not precede those who have
fallen asleep. For the Lord himself will descend from heaven
with a cry of command, with the archangel's call, and with the
sound of the trumpet of God. And the dead in Christ will rise
first, then we who are alive, who are left, shall be caught up
together with them in the clouds to meet the Lord in the air;
and so we shall always be with the Lord. Therefore comfort
one another with these words.—I Thessalonians 4:13-18.

(Then the minister may offer a prayer, closing with
this benediction:)

The grace of the Lord Jesus Christ and the love of God
and the fellowship of the Holy Spirit be with you all. Amen.
—II Corinthians 13:14.

35

III

(Standing at the head of the casket in the cemetery the minister may read:)

And I heard a voice from the throne saying, "Behold the dwelling of God is with men. He will dwell with them, and they shall be his people, and God himself will be with them; he will wipe away every tear from their eyes, and death shall be no more, neither shall there be mourning, nor crying, nor pain any more, for the former things have passed away."

And he who sat upon the throne said, "Behold, I make all things new." Also he said, "Write this, for these words are trustworthy and true." And he said to me, "It is done! I am the Alpha and the Omega, the beginning and the end. To the thirsty I will give water without price from the fountain of the water of life. He who conquers shall have this heritage, and I will be his God and he shall be my son."—Revelation 21:3-7.

(Then the minister may offer a prayer, or read an appropriate poem, and close with this benediction:)

And the peace of God, which passes all understanding, will keep your hearts and your minds in Christ Jesus. Amen.—Philippians 4:7.

A SERVICE FOR CREMATION

(When a service is conducted at a crematory, any of the preceding orders may be used; but the words of committal may be as follows:)

Forasmuch as it has pleased Almighty God to take unto Himself, the soul of our departed ...., we bear .... body to this place prepared for it; that ashes may return to ashes, dust to dust, and the imperishable spirit, refined as by fire, may be forever with the Lord.

36

A SERVICE FOR BURIAL AT SEA

(One of the preceding services may be used, then the
following committal is recommended:)

Forasmuch as it has pleased Almighty God to take out of
the world the soul of our departed ...., we therefore
commit .... body to the deep; looking for the resurrection
of the dead and the life eternal through our Lord Jesus Christ
at whose coming in glorious majesty, the moaning sea shall
give up her dead; our mortal bodies shall be made like unto
his glorious body—and the sea shall be no more.

(Then may follow the Lord's Prayer.)

FOR A SERVICE AT A *at grave*
MAUSOLEUM

Within this mansion of the dead
    We lay a form to rest,
A form a friend has tenanted
    And love and joy have blest.

The body shall return to dust
    According to the Word,
The spirit fellowships the just
    And Jesus Christ, our Lord.

Though Death reign here in stern array,
    Our faith to God we give:
While steel and stone and flesh decay,
    The soul with him shall live.

So we commit us all to God,
    Master of death and change,
And He will bring us to our friends
    Through loving ways and strange.
                —Amen.

                    — Chauncey R. Piety

A SERVICE FOR TEMPORARY BURIAL

(When the body has been temporarily deposited in a vault, use one of the preceding services; let the words of committal be as follows:)

Forasmuch as it has pleased Almighty God to remove from the world, the soul of our ...., we lay .... body here to rest a little while; then to be buried in the ground; then shall the dust return to dust as it was but the spirit returns to God who gave it.

A SERVICE FOR AN OCCASION WHEN THE BODY IS TAKEN AWAY

(If the body is taken away for burial elsewhere, these words may be used:)

We now commit the body of our departed friend and neighbor to those friends who will convey it to another community, there to find its rest in the bosom of Mother Earth— His spirit has returned to God, our Father, who gave it.

ADDITIONAL BENEDICTIONS FOR USE AT THE GRAVE

(To allow the minister a choice.)

And now as we leave here the form of the beloved, we pray for the comfort of our Father and our Lord Jesus Christ and of the Holy Spirit to be with you and all who sorrow. In His name we pray. Amen.

Leaving our dead in the hands of our All-Loving Father, we pray for His strength that we may endure, and His guidance that we may find the way. May the Grace of our Lord Jesus Christ, the Comfort of the Holy Spirit, keep your hearts until the day of the glad reunion with loved ones who have gone on before. Amen.

The Lord bless you, and keep you;
The Lord make his face to shine upon you,
    and be gracious unto you;
The Lord lift up his countenance upon you,
    and give you peace. Amen.
        —Numbers 6:24-26.

Thanks be to God, who gives us the victory through our Lord Jesus Christ. Therefore, my beloved brethren be steadfast, immovable, always abounding in the work of the Lord, knowing that in the Lord your labor is not in vain. In His name. Amen.   —I Corinthians 15:57, 58.

Now to him who by the power at work within us is able to do far more abundantly than all that we ask or think, to him be glory in the church and in Christ Jesus to all generations, for ever and ever. Amen.   —Ephesians 3:20.

The grace of the Lord Jesus Christ be with your spirit. Amen.   —Philippians 4:23.

A BRIEF SERVICE FOR HOME, OR CHURCH, OR FUNERAL HOME OR AT THE GRAVESIDE

When the funeral is held in the home, or funeral home, the minister should take his place at the head of the casket where possible. When the service is in the Church he may meet the casket at the door and precede it up the aisle; and, when the service is in the cemetery, he should meet the casket as it is removed from the funeral-ambulance and precede it to the grave.

Standing beside the casket at the home, or funeral home, or in the church, or at the grave the minister may say:

"Hear ye the word of the Lord! Comfort your hearts with these words. I am the resurrection and the life; he who believes in me, though he die, yet shall he live."

"I know that my redeemer lives, and at last he will stand upon the earth; and after my skin has been thus destroyed, then without my flesh I shall see God, whom I shall see on my side, and my eyes shall behold, and not another."—"The Lord gave, and the Lord has taken away; blessed be the name of the Lord."

GOD THE REFUGE OF HIS PEOPLE

God is our refuge and strength, a very present help in trouble. Therefore, we will not fear though the earth should change, though the mountains shake in the heart of the sea; though its waters roar and foam, though the mountains tremble with its tumult. There is a river whose streams make glad the city of God, the holy habitation of the Most High. God is in the midst of her, she shall not be moved; God will help her right early. The nations rage, the kingdoms totter; he utters his voice, the earth melts. The Lord of hosts is with us; the God of Jacob is our refuge. Come, behold the works of the Lord, how he has wrought desolations in the earth. He makes wars to cease to the end of the earth; he breaks the bow, and shatters the spear, he burns the chariots with fire! "Be still, and know that I am God. I am exalted among the nations, I am exalted in the earth!" The Lord of hosts is with us; the God of Jacob is our refuge.—Psalm 46.

GOD'S ETERNITY AND MAN'S TRANSITORY NATURE

(A Prayer of Moses, the man of God.)

Lord, thou has been our dwelling place in all generations. Before the mountains were brought forth, or ever thou hadst formed the earth and the world, from everlasting to everlasting thou art God. Thou turnest man back to the dust, and sayest, "Turn back, O children of men!" For a thousand years in thy sight are but as yesterday when it is past, or as a watch in the night. Thou dost sweep men away; they are like a dream, like grass which is renewed in the morning: in the morning it flourishes and is renewed; in the evening it fades and withers. For we are consumed by thy anger; by thy wrath we are overwhelmed. Thou hast set our iniquities before thee, our secret sins in the light of thy countenance. For all our days pass away under thy wrath, our years come to an end like a sigh. The years of our life are threescore and ten, or even by reason of strength fourscore; yet their span is but toil and trouble; they are soon gone and we fly away. Who considers the power of thy anger, and thy wrath according to the fear of thee? So teach us to number our days that we may get a heart of wisdom. Return, O Lord! How long? Have pity on thy servants! Satisfy us in the morning with thy steadfast love that we may rejoice and be glad all our days. Make us glad as many days as thou hast afflicted us, and as many years as we have seen evil. Let the work be manifest to thy servants, and thy glorious power to their children. Let the favor of the Lord our God be upon us, and establish thou the work of our hands upon us, yea, the work of our hands establish thou it.—Psalm 90.

SECURITY FOR HIM WHO TRUSTS IN THE LORD

He who dwells in the shelter of the Most High, who abides in the shadow of the Almighty, will say to the Lord, "My refuge and my fortress; my God, in whom I trust." For he will deliver you from the snare of the fowler and from the deadly pestilence; he will cover you with his pinions, and under his wings you will find refuge; his faithfulness is a shield and buckler. You will not fear the terror of the night, nor the arrow that flies by day, nor the pestilence that stalks in the darkness, nor the destruction that wastes at noonday. A thousand may fall at your side, ten thousand at your right hand; but it will not come near you. You will only look with your eyes and see the recompense of the wicked. Because you have made the Lord your refuge, the Most High your habitation, no evil shall befall you, no scourge come near your tent. For he will give his angels charge of you to guard you in all your ways. On their hands they will bear you up, lest you dash your foot against a stone. You will tread on the lion and the adder, the young lion and the serpent you will trample under foot. Because he cleaves to me in love, I will deliver him; I will protect him because he knows my name. When he calls to me I will answer him; I will be with him in trouble, I will rescue him and honor him. With long life I will satisfy him, and show him my salvation.—Psalm 91.

SUGGESTED FORMS ADAPTED FOR SERVICE
AT THE CHURCH

(After the body has been taken to its place before the chancel or pulpit the minister shall say:)

I am the resurrection and the life; he who believes in me, though he die, yet shall he live, and whoever lives and believes in me shall never die.—John 11:25, 26.

Blessed be the God and Father of our Lord Jesus Christ, the Father of mercies and God of all comfort, who comforts us in all our affliction, so that we may be able to comfort those who are in any affliction, with the comfort with which we ourselves are comforted by God.—II Corinthians 1:3, 4.

(Then the minister shall say:)

Let us pray.

(The prayer should be full of sympathy for the bereaved and uttered in all sincerity.)

Appropriate hymns are full of comfort, if rightly sung. Usually sing only two stanzas. Some very effective funeral services have been conducted without any singing—just the musical prelude and postlude consisting of well-chosen hymns.

Read the Scriptures freely and let your words be few.

There is growing sentiment among ministers to discourage profusion of flowers at funerals in favor of suggesting to sympathizers that some gift to the church, or cause in which the deceased had an active interest be made.

It may be noted that "public viewing of the remains tends to emphasize the mortal and material rather than the triumph of the spirit."

"Church, military and lodge funerals should not be intermingled." Simplicity, privacy and dignity should prevail.

42

CLASSIFIED SELECTIONS OF SCRIPTURE

(1) GENERAL SELECTIONS

Psalm 23 (See page 24)

Man that is born of woman is of few days, and full of trouble. He comes forth like a flower, and withers; he flees like a shadow, and continues not. Job 14:1, 2.

As for man, his days are like grass; he flourishes like a flower of the field; for the wind passes over it, and it is gone, and its place knows it no more. But the steadfast love of the Lord is from everlasting to everlasting upon those who fear him, and his righteousness to children's children, to those who keep his covenant and remember to do his commandments. —Psalm 103:15-18.

Psalm 90:1-9 (See page 41)

Truly, truly, I say to you, the hour is coming, and now is, when the dead will hear the voice of the Son of God, and those who hear will live. For as the Father has life in himself, so he has granted the Son also to have life in himself, and has given him authority to execute judgment, because he is the Son of man. Do not marvel at this; for the hour is coming when all who are in the tombs will hear his voice, and come forth, those who have done good, to the resurrection of life, and those who have done evil to the resurrection of judgment. —John 5:25-29.

(2) FOR FUNERAL SERVICES OF A CHILD

(It is quite appropriate for the body to lie in state in the home, church, chapel or funeral home for at least an hour prior to the service; then the casket is closed and remains closed.)

(At the beginning of the service the minister may say:)

"Comfort your hearts with these words."

(Use several selections of Scripture.)

The Lord answer you in the day of trouble! The name of the God of Jacob protect you! May he send you help from the sanctuary, and give you support from Zion!—Psalm 20: 1, 2.

Lord, let me know my end, and what is the measure of my days; let me know how fleeting my life is! Behold thou hast made my days a few hand-breadths, and my lifetime is as nothing in thy sight. Surely every man stands as a mere breath! —Psalm 39:4, 5.

But when David saw that his servants were whispering together, David perceived that the child was dead; and David said to his servants, "Is the child dead?" They said, "He is dead." Then David arose from the earth, and washed, and anointed himself, and changed his clothes; and he went into the house of the Lord, and worshipped; he then went to his own house; and when he asked, they set food before him, and he ate. Then his servants said to him, "What is this thing that you have done? You fasted and wept for the child while he was alive; but when the child died, you arose and ate food." He said, "While the child was still alive, I fasted and wept; for I said, 'Who knows whether the Lord will be gracious to me, that the child may live.' But now he is dead; why should I fast? Can I bring him back again? I shall go to him, but he will not return to me."—II Samuel 12:19-23.

The children were brought to him that he might lay his hands on them and pray. The disciples rebuked the people; but Jesus said, "Let the children come to me, and do not hinder them; for to such belongs the kingdom of heaven." And he laid his hands on them and went away.—Matthew 19:13-15.

And they were bringing children to him, that he might touch them; and the disciples rebuked them. But when Jesus saw it he was indignant and said to them, "Let the children come to me, do not hinder them; for to such belongs the kingdom of God. Truly, I say to you, whoever does not reecive the kingdom of God like a little child shall not enter it." And he took them in his arms and blessed them, laying his hands upon them.—Mark 10:13-16.

(Additional selections of Scripture may be chosen from this list:)
Matthew 18:1-6, 10-14
Luke 18:15, 16   Psalm 103:13, 14
II Corinthians 1:3, 4   Isaiah 40:10, 11
Revelation 21:2-4   Jeremiah 31:15, 16a
Psalm 27:13, 14   Nahum 1:7

(3) FOR FUNERAL OF A YOUTH

In the morning sow your seed, and at evening withhold not your hand; for you do not know which will prosper, this or that, or whether both alike will be good. Light is sweet, and it is pleasant for the eyes to behold the sun. For if a man lives many years, let him rejoice in them all; but let him remember that the days of darkness will be many. All that comes is vanity. Rejoice, O young man, in your youth, and let your heart cheer you in the days of your youth; walk in the ways of your heart and the sight of your eyes. But know that for all these things God will bring you into judgment. Remove vexations from your mind, and put away pain from your body; for youth and the dawn of life are vanity. —Ecclesiastes 11:6-10.

Remember also your creator in the days of your youth, before the evil days come, and the years draw nigh, when you will say, "I have no pleasure in them."—Ecclesiastes 12:1.

Then the kingdom of heaven shall be compared to ten maidens who took their lamps and went to meet the bridegroom. Five of them were foolish and five were wise. For when the foolish took their lamps, they took no oil with them; but the wise took flasks of oil with their lamps. As the bridegroom was delayed, they all slumbered and slept. But at midnight there was a cry, "Behold, the bridegroom! Come out to meet him." Then all those maidens rose and trimmed their lamps. And the foolish said to the wise, "Give us some of your oil, for our lamps are going out." But the wise replied, "Perhaps there will not be enough for us and for you; go rather to the dealers and buy for yourselves." And while they went to buy, the bridegroom came, and those who were ready went in with him to the marriage feast; and the door was shut. Afterward the other maidens came also, saying, "Lord, lord, open to us." But he replied, "Truly, I say to you I do not know you." Watch therefore for you know neither the day nor the hour.—Matthew 25:1-13.

Peace I leave with you; my peace I give to you; not as the world gives do I give to you. Let not your hearts be troubled, neither let them be afraid.—John 14:27.

(4) FOR FUNERAL OF A MATURE PERSON

One dies in full prosperity, being wholly at ease and secure, his body full of fat and the marrow of his bones moist. Another dies in bitterness of soul, never having tasted of good. They lie down alike in the dust.—Job 21:23-26a.

Yet God prolongs the life of the mighty by his power; they rise up when they despair of life. He gives them security, and they are supported; and his eyes are upon their ways. They are exalted a little while, and then are gone; they wither and fade like the mallow; they are cut off like the heads of grain.—Job 24:22-24.

But of that day or that hour no one knows, not even the angels in heaven, nor the Son, but only the Father. Take heed, watch; for you do not know when the time will come. It is like a man going on a journey, when he leaves home and puts his servants in charge, each with his work, and commands the doorkeeper to be on the watch. Watch therefore—for you do not know when the master of the house will come, in the evening, or at midnight, or at cockcrow, or in the morning—lest he come suddenly and find you asleep. And what I say to you I say to all: Watch.—Mark 13:32-37.

Come now, you who say, "Today or tomorrow we will [go] into such and such a town and spend a year there and trade and get gain"; whereas you do not know about tomorrow. What is your life? For you are a mist that appears for a little time and then vanishes. Instead you ought to say, "If the Lord wills, we shall live and we shall do this or that."—James 4: 13-15.

(5) FOR FUNERAL OF THE AGED

Our years come to an end like a sigh. The years of our life are three score and ten, or if by reason of strength forescore; yet their span is but toil and trouble; they are soon gone and we fly away. Let the favor of the Lord our God be upon us, and establish thou the work of our hands upon us, yea, the work of our hands establish thou it.—Psalm 90:9, 10, 17.

A hoary head is a crown of glory; it is gained in a righteous life. He who is slow to anger is better than the mighty, and he who rules his spirit than he who takes a city.—Proverbs 16:31, 32.

Your eyes will see the king in his beauty; they will behold a land that stretches afar. For the Lord is our judge, the Lord is our ruler, the Lord is our king; he will save us.—Isaiah 33:17, 22.

(6) FOR FUNERAL OF A BELIEVER

Jesus said to her, "I am the resurrection and the life; he who believes in me, though he die, yet shall he live, and whoever lives and believes in me shall never die. Do you believe this?" She said to him, "Yes, Lord; I believe that you are the Christ, the Son of God, he who is coming into the world." —John 11:25-27.

But we would not have you ignorant, brethren, concerning those who are asleep, that you may not grieve as others do who have no hope. For since we believe that Jesus died and rose again, even so, through Jesus, God will bring with him those who have fallen asleep. For this we declare to you by the word of the Lord, that we who are alive, who are left until the coming of the Lord, shall not precede those who have fallen asleep. For the Lord himself will descend from heaven with a cry of command, with the archangel's call, and with the sound of the trumpet of God. And the dead in Christ shall rise first, then we who are alive, who are left, shall be caught up together with them in the clouds to meet the Lord in the air; and so we shall always be with the Lord. Therefore comfort one another with these words.—I Thessalonians 4:13-18.

And I heard a voice from heaven saying, "Write this: Blessed are the dead who die in the Lord henceforth." "Blessed indeed," says the Spirit, "that they may rest from their labors, for their deeds follow them."—Revelation 14:13.

Then I saw a new heaven and a new earth; for the first heaven and the first earth had passed away, and the sea was no more. And I saw the holy city, new Jerusalem, coming down out of heaven from God, prepared as a bride adorned for her husband; and I heard a great voice from the throne saying, "Behold, the dwelling of God is with men. He will dwell with them and they shall be his people, and God himself will be with them; he will wipe away every tear from their eyes, and death shall be no more, neither shall there be mourning nor crying nor pain any more, for the former things have passed away."—Revelation 21:1-4.

BRIEF OUTLINES FOR FUNERAL MESSAGES

In all probability the minister of a small or rural church will address more people at a funeral than on any other occasion. It is very essential that memorial messages be well prepared and appropriate. To give a few suggestions toward effective messages the following outlines are offered. There is a growing trend toward the omission of funeral sermons. Brief, personal messages are more appropriate.

EVENING COMES

Text: On that day when evening had come, he said to them, "Let us go across to the other side."—Mark 4:35.

1. Life is like a Day
   The early morning hours of babyhood—
   The morning of youth—
   High noon of maturity—
   Then evening comes, and the day ends.

2. Life is measured in deeds
   Not just the passing of time—
   Not merely money-making—
   Not fame or brilliance—

   Happy is he who goes about doing good.
3. As Evening comes we recall the activities of the day that has passed
   We see in clearer perspective the great moral principles of life—
   Things of real worth stand out—
   The Christian graces take on their true meaning.
       (See Galatians 5:22, 23.)

THE END OF THE WAY

Text: Lord, let me know my end, and what is the measure of my days.—Psalm 39:4.

As life draws toward a close it is quite natural for one to talk about the end of the way. There is the persistent question—When will the end come? One can recall the past and dream of what lies ahead.

1. The backward look
   What has been achieved?
   What things have been most important?

2. The look beyond the end
   When death is near we think of the beyond.
   The realities of life come into view—
       Illustration: The light in the window

he end of the earthly highway gives one confidence in
    immortality
Life is continuous
Death is only a transition, a phase
The old moorings fade away as we dream of the heavenly
    home.

A PREPARED PLACE

Text: "I go to prepare a place for you."—John 14:2.

How often the fourteenth chapter of John has been read in times
when comfort was sorely needed! Throughout His ministry Jesus went
ahead.

1. The Master knows the Heavenly Home
   He came from heaven to earth—
   He taught men how to prepare for life—
   He inspired them to look toward the heavenly home.

2. The Christian Life is to be at Home with God
   "Our souls are restless until they find rest in Him"—
   To live at our best here is to be prepared to live over there—
   The heavenly home is a prepared place for those who are
       prepared to enjoy it—

3. Home is more than a place
   It is a fellowship of loved ones—
   It takes continuous effort to attain—
   It means companionship with Christ—
   "I will come again and will take you to myself."—John 14:3b.

WHAT IS YOUR LIFE?

Text: She was full of good works and acts of charity.—Acts
9:36b.

The story of a life is told not in years but in deeds. Dorcas was
remembered for her good works and acts of charity.

1. Life is a Gift from God
   We breathe involuntarily—
   Our breath is in God's hands—
   Human life is marvelous—

2. Life is a Priceless Treasure
   More valuable than the whole world—
   To be guarded with utmost care—
   To be used for the noblest purposes—

3. A Perishable - Imperishable Trust
   Our physical selves suffer the ravages of time, sickness,
      accident—
   Our spiritual selves live on throughout eternity—
   Each is dependent upon the other—
   Life is like a spring, a brook, a river, an ocean, a vapor,
      rain—the cycle then begins over again—continuous.

READY AND WATCHING

Text: You also must be ready; for the Son of Man is coming at
an hour you do not expect.—Luke 12:40.

Every birth is the announcement of another death. Death is veiled
with mystery and draped in sadness.

1. Death comes to everyone
   Every day, every hour, every moment death comes to some-
      one—
   Death brings broken hearts, desolate homes, vacant chairs.
   Childhood, youth, maturity included.

2. The time is not known
   Jesus is the gardener—
   He may pluck the most fragrant flower—
   We are here but for a moment—

3. Let us be ready and watching
   A challenge to live nobly—
   A call to be prepared to live a long time but ready to go at
      any time.
   As we live so will death find us.

TOPICAL REFERENCES FOR FUNERAL MESSAGES

(These additional Scripture Selections for Funeral
Services may serve as a guide to choice of the most
appropriate readings for a given service.)

1. "He is Lent to the Lord."—I Samuel 1:28.
2. "The Lord Will Take Me Up."—Psalm 27:10.
3. "Bowed Down in Mourning."—Psalm 35:14.
4. "God in His Holy Habitation."—Psalm 68:5.
5. "They Are Soon Gone."—Psalm 90:10.
6. "Set Your House in Order."—II Kings 20:1.

7. "He Will Carry Nothing Away."—Psalm 49:17.
8. "Like a Shadow."—Job 14:1.
9. "The Lord Gave . . . Has Taken Away."—Job 1:21.
10. "As a Shock of Grain."—Job 5:26.
11. "A Little Child Shall Lead Them."—Isaiah 11:6.
12. "He Will Feed His Flock."—Isaiah 40:11.
13. "Precious in the Sight of the Lord."—Psalm 116:15.
14. "Memory of the Righteous."—Proverbs 10:7.
15. "He Enters into Peace."—Isaiah 57:2.
16. "Walked in Peace and Righteousness."—Malachi 2:6.
17. "Prepare to Meet Your God."—Amos 4:12.
18. "Blessed Are the Pure in Heart."—Matthew 5:8.
19. "I Will Give You Rest."—Matthew 11:28.
20. "Inherit the Kingdom."—Matthew 25:34.
21. "Who Will Roll Away the Stone "—Mark 16:2.
22. "Let Not Your Heart Be Troubled."—John 14:1.
23. "The Crown of Righteousness."—II Timothy 4:6-8.
24. "By Faith . . . A More Acceptable Sacrifice."—Hebrews 11:4.
25. "A House Not Made with Hands."—II Corinthians 5:1.

APPROPRIATE HYMNS AND POEMS

A FEW HYMNS SUITABLE FOR FUNERAL USE

Hymns for funeral use should abound in faith, hope, love. They should cause those present to have stronger faith, deeper consciousness of the presence of God, and lend a spirit of confidence. We have often used, in days gone by, songs of the more emotional type. Often these are used by family request. Certainly in a funeral service it is much better to stress positive qualities of character exemplified by the deceased and to sing hymns of faith, noble purpose, challenge, comfort. Here are a few strongly recommended hymns and songs—

"Abide with Me."—Lyte-Monk.
"Our God, Our Help in Ages Past."—Watts-Croft.
"Praise to the Lord, the Almighty."—Neander.
"The Lord Is My Shepherd."—Montgomery-Koschat.
"My Faith Looks Up to Thee."—Palmer-Mason.
"All the Way My Saviour Leads Me."—Crosby-Lowry.
"Come, Ye Disconsolate."—Moore-Hastings-Webbe.
"Jesus, Saviour Pilot Me."—Hopper-Gould.
"Great Is Thy Faithfulness."—Chisolm-Runyon.
"How Strong and Sweet My Father's Care."—Murray.

"This Is My Father's World."—Babcock-Sheppard.
"What a Friend We Have in Jesus."—Scriven-Converse.
"Lead Kindly Light."—Newman-Dykes.
"A Charge to Keep I Have."—Wesley-Mason.
"The Lord's Prayer."—Malotte.
"The Twenty-Third Psalm."—Malotte.

I AM LIVING NOW TO LIVE AGAIN

I am living now to live again,
    For life is too good to close;
As the body breaks with the weight of years,
    The soul the stronger grows.

I am living now to live again,
    For God within leads on
From dream to deed, from deed to dream,
    And shall when earth is gone.

I am living now to live again
    As spirit values will;
For the soul I build of spirit stuff
    No death can ever kill.

I am living now to live again,
    If a God of love there be;
For my love in His love cannot die
    In all eternity.

I am living now to live again—
    Flesh and bone will turn to dust;
But my soul, a part of the eternal God,
    Can live, will live, it must.

—Chauncey R. Piety

GOD HAS BEEN GOOD TO ME

God has been good to me. To tell in part demands new words.
    His gracious power in so many ways
    Has blessed me through long years of happy days.
    I have not eloquence to voice his praise;
I can but say with grateful heart "God has been good to me."

—Author Unknown

THE BREAD THAT GIVETH STRENGTH

The bread that giveth strength I want to give,
The water pure that bids the thirsty live;
I want to help the fainting day by day,
I'm sure I shall not pass again this way.

I want to give the oil of joy for tears,
The faith to conquer crowding doubts and fears;
Beauty for ashes may I give alway,
I'm sure I shall not pass again this way.

I want to give good measure, running o'er,
And into angry hearts I want to pour
The answer soft that turneth wrath away,
I'm sure I shall not pass again this way.

I want to give to others hope and faith;
I want to do all that the Master saith;
I want to live aright from day to day,
I'm sure I shall not pass again this way.

—Author Unknown
(May be used as a hymn.)

We live in deeds, not years;
    In thoughts, not breaths;
He lives most who thinks most,
    Feels the noblest, acts the best.
—Selected

AT EIGHTY-FOUR

A true old age comes as a dream,
    Like slowing currents in a stream;
Time softens dread, that yields to hope
    Which bears one down an easy slope.

Fourscore and four are not the goal,
    They are a part, but not the whole;
Perhaps this is a mountain crest,
    Before the ocean in the west.

And if some steep descents await,
    We sooner reach the golden gate;
Then we shall pause with restful mind,
    And wait for you who come behind.
—Clinton Lockhart

HOLD HIGH THE TORCH

Hold high the torch!
You did not light its glow—
'Twas given you by other hands, you know,
'Tis yours to keep it burning bright,
Yours to pass on when you no more need light;
For there are other feet that we must guide,
And other forms go marching by our side;
Their eyes are watching every smile and tear
And efforts which we think are not worth while,
Are sometimes just the very help they need,
Actions to which their souls would give most heed.

—Author Unknown

THE HUMAN TOUCH

'Tis the human touch in this world that counts,
    The touch of your hand with mine,
Which means far more to the fainting heart
    Than shelter and bread and wine.

For shelter is gone when the night is o'er,
    And bread lasts only a day;
But the touch of the hand and the sound of your voice
    Sings on in the soul alway.

—Author Unknown

THE PASSING OF A FRIEND

Far from the noise of city streets,
    From pageantry and show
In ways of quietness and peace
    Her life was made to flow.

As Martha made the hearth all bright
    And shining with love's ray,
So she it was who trimmed the lamps
    To light the heart's highway.

Her work is done, the task is o'er,
    Nor will the spirit roam,
For she has gone to make more dear
    Another place called Home.

—Dorothy Talbott Foster

WHEN THE TRUMPET SOUNDS

When the trumpet sounds for me to go,
I'll hear it full,
I'll feel the pull
Against the fragile cord of life
And when it snaps, God grant the star
Which guides the flight of feeble wings
Across the purple tide of strife
May not be dimmed by dreams that jar,
The dreams that cling to passing things—
To hold to hands that I will know
Must wait awhile.
No, with a smile,

A knowing glance, I'll bid "goodnight."
But I shall linger somewhere near
To say "good morning," and a prayer
As dear ones end the lonely flight
Across the seas of this dark sphere,
Across the heavy tides of care,
Across the gulfs where Gabriels blow,
When all defeat
The tomb and meet

Upon the plain where love unveils,
Together, we shall travel on
Up starry aisles, with joy unfurled;
On up the rising rainbow trails
Until we swing into the dawn
Of wisdom's love illumined world.

—Margie B. Boswell

The soul on earth is an immortal guest,
Compelled to starve at an unreal feast;
A spark which upward tends by nature's force,
A stream divided from its parent source,
A drop dissevered from the boundless sea,
A moment parted from eternity,
A pilgrim panting for the rest to come;
An exile anxious for his native home.

—Hannah More

LEAN ON THE LORD

Lean on the Lord in thy sorrow;
  Lean on the strength of His arm;
Trust in the word of His promise;
  He will not suffer you harm.
He knows thy troubles aforetime;
  That pave the way for His grace;
He waiteth now for thine asking;
  Why stand aloof from His face?

(REFRAIN)

Lean on the Lord who is waiting above,
Lean on the arm of His infinite love.

Lean on the Lord in thy sorrow;
  Lean on the strength of His might;
Trust in the fullness of mercy;
  He will direct thee aright.
He will not fail in thy trial:
  His are the sources of love;
He is now waiting in heaven,
  Bending with blessing above.

(REFRAIN)

—Clinton Lockhart

SUCCESS

If, after I have crossed the great divide,
  My hovering spirit, lingering near by, hears
The comments that my recent passing caused;
  I'd want no sorrow ringing in my ears.

But I should like to hear the low-pitched voice
  Of one whom I had touched in passing say,
"My heart has more of sunshine than before,
  Because, in life, her footsteps came my way."

If I could know that I had been the means,
  Some lonely life to cheer or lift or bless,
As I walked down the long and rugged trail;
  Then I would feel that I had known success.

—Leola Littrell

57

HOW BEAUTIFUL TO BE WITH GOD!

How beautiful to be with God,
　　When earth is fading like a dream,
And from this mist-encircled shore
　　We launch upon the unknown stream!
No doubt, no fear, no anxious care
　　But comforted by staff and rod,
In the faith-brightened hour of death
　　How beautiful to be with God!

Beyond the partings and the pains,
　　Beyond the sighing and the tears,
Oh, beautiful to be with God
　　Through all the endless, blessed years—
To see His face, to hear His voice,
　　To know Him better day by day,
And love Him as the flowers love light,
　　And serve Him as immortals may.

　　　　　　　　　　—Author Unknown

BANKRUPT

One midnight, deep in starlight still,
　　I dreamed that I received this bill:
(.................................. in account with Life):
　　Five thousand breathless dawns all new,
Five thousand flowers fresh with dew;
　　Five thousand sunsets wrapped in gold;
One million snowflakes served ice-cold;
　　Five quiet friends; one baby's love;
One white-mad sea with clouds above;
　　One hundred music haunted dreams
Of moon-drenched roads and hurrying streams;
　　Of prophesying winds, and trees;
Of silent stars and browsing bees;
　　One June night in a fragrant wood;
One heart that loved and understood.
　　I wondered when I waked at day,
How—how in God's name—I could pay!

　　　　　　　　　　—Courtlandt Sayers

WORSHIP

Thy presence, Spirit God, doth fill this place;
   This mellow glow doth give us inner sight
To know, though all around is black as night,
   That thou art here. And so we seek thy face.
Out there a troubled world moves on its way,
   Out there are toils and cares and bitter tears;
But here in one brief hour we lose our fears,
   And find our darkness, Lord, is turned to day.
Here quiet music bids our sorrows cease,
   Here sacred stillness bids us list to thee;
Here eyes unseeing, blind, are made to see,
   Here questing spirits find eternal peace.
Why, then, should burdens fill our lives with care,
   When thou art here and we may kneel in prayer?

—John Calvin Slemp

DEATH

The world recedes; it disappears;
   Heav'n opens on my eyes; my ears
With sound seraphic ring:
   Lend, lend your wings! I mount! I fly!
O Grave! where is thy victory,
   O Death! where is thy sting?

What is death? Oh! What is death?
   'Tis slumber to the weary—
   'Tis rest to the forlorn—
   'Tis shelter to the dreary—
   'Tis peace amid the storm—
   'Tis the entrance to our home—
   'Tis the passage to that God
Who bids his children come,
   When their weary course is trod,
Such is death! Yes, such is death.

—Anonymous

HE LIVED A LIFE

What was his creed?
   I do not know his creed, I only know
That here below, he walked the common road
   And lifted many a load, lightened the task,
Brightened the day for others toiling on a weary way;
   This, his only meed; I do not know his creed.

What was his creed? I never heard him speak
   Of visions rapturous, of Alpine peak
Of doctrine, dogma, new or old;
   But this I know, he was forever bold
To stand alone, to face the challenge of each day,
   And live the truth, so far as he could see—
The truth that evermore makes free.

His creed? I care not what his creed;
   Enough that never yielded he to greed,
But served a brother in his daily need;
   Plucked many a thorn and planted many a flower;
Glorified the service of each hour;
   Had faith in God, himself, and fellow-men;
Perchance he never thought in terms of creed;
   I only know he lived a life, in deed!

—H. N. Fifer

GOOD-BYE, TILL MORNING COMES

"Good-bye, till morning comes again,"
   We part, if part we must, with pain,
But night is short and hope is sweet,
   Faith fills our hearts, and wings our feet;
And so we sing the old refrain,
   "Good-bye, till morning comes again."
"Good-bye, till morning comes again,"
   The thought of death brings weight of pain.
But could we know how short the night
   That falls and hides them from our sight,
Our hearts would sing the old refrain,
   "Good-bye, till morning comes again."

—Author Unknown

CROSSING THE BAR

Sunset and evening star
    And one clear call for me!
And may there be no moaning of the bar,
    When I put out to sea.

But such atide as moving seems asleep,
    Too full for sound and foam,
When that which drew from out the boundless deep
    Turns again home.

Twilight and evening bell,
    And after that the dark!
And may there be no sadness of farewell,
    When I embark;

For tho' from out our bourne of Time and Place
    The flood may bear me far,
I hope to see my Pilot face to face
    When I have crost the bar.

                    —Alfred Lord Tennyson

BE STILL

("Be still and know that I am God."
                Psalm 46:10a.)
O, restless, troubled soul, BE STILL, and know
    That He is God, the Lord. That He will be
Your strength and stay. Then, all the winds which blow
    In raging tempest, over land and sea,
Cannot upset the deep serenity
    That dwells within . . . nor quench the constant flow
Pouring from God's white throne, effulgently,
    When we ARE STILL . . . and learn His will to know.

BE STILL! and know that God will lead us on
    In paths we cannot see; that He will guide
Our faltering steps. We shall not walk alone.
    He will be near, whatever may be tide.
In the mad rush of life, it is His will
    That we should sometimes listen, and BE STILL.

                    —Catherine Nunley Wilson

LIFT YOUR LIFE

In every life some gleaming tallness lifts
In silent beauty like a shaft of light;
High up, and higher yet, until it rifts
The veil of darkness with its vaulting height.
The clangor of the market place is lost,
The clamoring of crowded concourse dies,
A dream is born from out life's holocaust
As one sure hope leaps upward to the skies.

A life was meant to bless humanity . . .
Though heavy clouds may press you to the earth
A conflict faced and won, is to be free,
That is a certainty of ageless worth.
So lift that lighted shaft God gave to you
And with it, find your tract of shining blue!

—Nora Beth Main.

GOD WALKS IN THE GARDEN

God walks in the garden,
And the gloom and the dark
Change to the lights
Of a heavenly park.

God walks in the garden
And the delicate hues
Of iris and jonquil
And the brittle blues
Of harebell and larkspur
Mingle and blend
In a glorious pattern
Which has no end.

God walks in the garden—
He treads up and down;
And each bud and blossom
Lifts a star-crown
Fragile, filigreed
But of infinite worth
To Him who fashioned
This beautiful earth.

—-Margie B. Boswell

62

A COMMITTAL SERVICE POEM

According to the eternal plan,
   The body returns to the earth as it was,
And the spirit to God who gave it.
   Of all that is material we say,
"Earth to earth, ashes to ashes, dust to dust":
   But to the spirit we cry:
"Now thou art free,
   Free from pain and sickness and sorrow.
Free from all physical handicaps,
   Free to dream and sing and work and love.
Free to greet old friends and new
   And Jesus Christ,
And to adventure with them forever."
   Therefore we say,
"Good-bye, good-bye until tomorrow." Amen.
                    —Chauncey R. Piety

GOOD NIGHT

Warm summer sun,
   Shine kindly here.
Warm southern wind,
   Blow softly here.
Green sod above,
   Lie light, lie light,
Good night, dear heart,
   Good night, good night.

                —Robert Richardson

A LIFE WELL LIVED

So live, that when thy summons comes to join
   The innumerable caravan, which moves
To that mysterious realm, where each shall take
   His chamber in the silent halls of death,
Thou go not, like a quarry-slave at night,
   Scourged to his dungeon, but, sustained and soothed
By an unfaltering trust, approach thy grave
   Like one who wraps the drapery of his couch
About him and lies down to pleasant dreams.
                —William Cullen Bryant

MY BODY

My body is a bit of dust
  In which the "I" of me resides
For the time of earthly tenantry;
  When I cease to need it,
It will return to earth and be no more.

The "I" of me will return to God
  Who gave me this bit of body
Through which to try my powers.
  In it I have learned the lessons
Of weight, extent, direction and control;
  And of suffering, sorrow, and self denial.

These skills become part of me,
  The sense of them can never leave me.
They are mine for all eternity.
  They enable me to enjoy my house of dust,
And through it to glorify my Creator,
  Here on earth as well as in Heaven.

Thus, I have loved my body,
  As if it were eternal,
Knowing well that it is not so,
  I do not wish to part with my body,
Though it is old and worn and weak,
  But God has promised me a new body
That will never grow tired, or sick, or old!

How wonderful! I think I will go see
  What skills and lessons I can learn
Through the use of this new body.

You who know me here
  Will know me there when you come,
For that spiritual body will be "like"
  My earthly "bit of dust," only it will be
Free of pain, and know no Death!

                    —Bertha Mason Fuller

VOICELESS LANGUAGE

On mountain or in valley,
On plain or tumbling sea,
God speaks a voiceless language
To you . . . to me.

On ether waves, transparent
And thin a crystal glass,
The flame-winged phrases flutter
And fall. Though quick they pass

Beyond the rim of hearing,
Man may identify
The message clear and certain,
As it skims lightly by.

This is the wordless language—
The language of God's love—
Which everyone may master,
And everyone may prove.
                    —Margie B. Boswell

Chapter III

THE MINISTER SERVES THROUGH
SPECIAL OCCASIONS

A SERVICE FOR LEADERSHIP DAY
RECOGNITION AND INSTALLATION OF CHURCH
SCHOOL WORKERS

(This type of service may be very simple, or more elaborate, depending on what you seek to accomplish. It may be extended to include all officers and leaders in every department within the life of the Church. The following is limited to recognition and installation of Church school workers. In any event this service should be impressive and sincere.)

INSTRUMENTAL PRELUDE: (Use a meditative number)

(All worshippers should enter the Sanctuary in silence, be seated, and let the mind dwell upon God as the source of all truth; upon God's fullest expression of love through Jesus Christ. Each one should recall and thank God for teachers who have been influential in his life.)

CALL TO WORSHIP: (Minister) II Timothy 2:15, then say—

As disciples of Christ, we are seeking in this hour a closer fellowship with Him and with each other. We desire to honor those who have contributed to the development of our lives, and to install those who have been chosen to carry the torch of leadership in our Church School. We would today renew our vows of Christian leadership.

HYMN: "Saviour, More Than Life to Me," or "He Leadeth Me; O Blessed Thought."

(Standing)

A MOMENT OF THOUGHTFUL SILENCE: (Guided by minister)

PRAYER: (By minister or elder)

CHORAL RESPONSE: (Youth choir)

SCRIPTURE READING: II Corinthians 3:1-6, 17-18 (By a woman teacher)

SPECIAL MUSIC: (A hymn solo full of challenge)

ROLL CALL OF CHURCH SCHOOL STAFF: (Superintendent or Director of Christian Education)

(As the names of teachers and officers are read each one will stand and remain standing until the roll has been completed.)

67

HYMN OF CONSECRATION: "O Master, Let Me Walk With Thee," or "I Bind My Heart This Tide"

MESSAGE: "I Would Rather Be" (Minister)

SERVICE OF INSTALLATION: (All teachers and officers will stand)

Minister: You have been called to serve in the school of this congregation. This is your opportunity. I charge each and every one of you to pray, work, grow in effectiveness, and to dedicate yourselves in this hour to the work committed to your care and keeping.

Officers and Teachers: Before God and in the presence of our fellow Christians, we do covenant together to give of our time, our talents, and our treasure toward the fulfillment of all requirements of the several positions to which we have been assigned. Following in the footsteps of the Master Teacher we will seek guidance from the throne of God, and strive to enter with understanding into the challenging demands of our calling.

(Congregation)

We agree to stand back of the officers and teachers of our Church school and pray that they may be guided into channels of greatest usefulness.

*PRAYER OF INSTALLATION: (An elder, or mature woman)

HYMN: "O Jesus, I Have Promised"

BENEDICTION: (unison)

Let the words of my mouth, and the meditation of my heart, be acceptable in thy sight, O Lord, my Strength and my Redeemer. Amen. —Psalm 19:14.

---

*NOTE: This service may be enlarged and enriched if desired. A litany of consecration would be very appropriate at this point.

PROCEDURE FOR LOCATION OF NEW CHURCH

It should be recognized at the very outset of this church building enterprise that local situations vary. Locating a new church in a rural, or small town area is quite different from a similar undertaking in a growing city. Only general directive procedures are offered on this page. For expert guidance secure a pamphlet on "How to Start a New Church" by Fred W. Michel, United Christian Missionary Society, 222 S. Downey Avenue, Indianapolis 7, Indiana.

SUGGESTED PROCEDURE

1. Provide for a New Church Committee—
   A small, representative committee (3 to 5),
   An interested, devoted group of people,
   People with sound business judgment.
2. Make clear the Responsibilities of the Committee—
   Discover the actual need,
   Determine the approximate cost,
   The initial cost—Operating cost for one year.
   Available resources—(financial)
3. Conduct a Community Survey—
   To discover personnel to be served,
   To find out population trends—today and through the years,
   To determine reasonable strategies to follow.
4. Choose a Site—
   Make sure of sufficient acreage,
   Transportation and parking facilities,
   Possibilities of growth.
5. Report Findings to Sponsoring Church
   Use maps, drawings, pictures,
   Give report on the complete study,
   State fully your reasons for recommendation of a chosen site.

NOTE: The headquarters office of your State, or National Board will be glad to offer expert guidance. Be sure of what you are doing then move forward in faith.

SERVICE OF GROUNDBREAKING
(At New Church Site)

CALL TO WORSHIP . . . . Minister

INVOCATION . . . .
Chairman of Official Board

DEDICATION OF SITE . . . . Minister

LEADER: Beloved in the Lord, we rejoice that God put it into the hearts of His people to break this ground to the glory of His name. I now set it apart for the building of First Christian Church. Let us, therefore, as we are assembled, solemnly dedicate this site to its proper and sacred uses.

To the glory of God, the Father, who has called us by His grace;

To the honor of His Son, who loved us and gave Himself for us;

To the praise of the Holy Spirit, who illuminates and sanctifies us,

PEOPLE: WE BREAK THIS GROUND.

LEADER: For the worship of God in prayer and praise; for the preaching of the everlasting gospel; for the celebration of the Lord's Supper,

PEOPLE: WE BREAK THIS GROUND.

LEADER: For the comfort of all who mourn; for strength to those who are tempted; for light for those who seek the way,

PEOPLE: WE BREAK THIS GROUND.

LEADER: For the hallowing of Family Life; for teaching and guiding the young; for the preaching ministry,

PEOPLE: WE BREAK THIS GROUND.

LEADER: For the conversion of sinners; for the promotion of righteousness; for the extension of the Kingdom of God,

PEOPLE: WE BREAK THIS GROUND.

LEADER: In the unity of the faith; in the bond of Christian Brotherhood; in charity and good will to all,

PEOPLE: WE BREAK THIS GROUND.

LEADER: In gratitude for the labors of all who love and serve this church; in loving remembrance of those who have finished their course; in the hope of a blessed immortality through Jesus Christ our Lord,

PEOPLE: WE BREAK THIS GROUND.

LEADER AND PEOPLE: We now, the people and congregation, compassed about with a great cloud of witnesses, grateful for our heritage, aware of the sacrifice of our fathers in the faith, confessing that apart from us their work cannot be made perfect, do dedicate ourselves anew to the worship and service of Almighty God, through Jesus Christ our Lord. Amen.

ACT OF UNITING THE PAST WITH THE PRESENT AND FUTURE: Second Secretary of the first organized Youth Work in First Christian Church, will present the representatives of the present Youth organizations with the Minutes of activities of the Young Peoples Christian Endeavor Society.

THE CHALLENGE OF THE PAST TO THE PRESENT AND FUTURE: Sponsor of the Christian Endeavor Society that won the State Banner at the Texas Christian Endeavor Convention, will present that Banner to the Representatives of today's Youth as a challenge to future accomplishments.

ACT OF GROUNDBREAKING: The following people will break ground as representatives of the Youth groups of today, acknowledging their indebtedness to those who have preceded them, and accepting the challenge to dedicate themslves to the worship and service of their Lord, Jesus Christ.

> Representative of the Older Young People
> President Senior Christian Youth Fellowship
> President Junior High Christian Youth Fellowship

PRAYER AND BENEDICTION
> (Chairman, Building Project Committee)

A CORNER STONE LAYING SERVICE

(Frequently it is desirable to mark the completion of the foundation of a new church building, by placing a corner stone with appropriate ceremony. Many variations in procedure, to match local situations, are possible. The following form is humbly submitted as a suggestion:)

Trumpet Call to Worship: (sounded on a brass instrument, or a quartet of instruments)—"Holy, Holy, Holy."

Opening statement by the minister:

We are met on this significant occasion to lay the corner stone of this church building. Thus do we give recognition to the first step in progress of material construction in the words of Isaiah—

> "Behold, I am laying in Zion for a foundation
> a stone, a tested stone, a precious cornerstone
> of a sure foundation . . . Give ear and hear my
> voice; harken, and hear my speech."—Isaiah
> 28:16, 23.

As we lay this corner stone let us look beyond things that are seen and remember that the Church of the living God has but one true corner stone—Jesus Christ—tried, precious, true.

Let us offer to God our humble prayer—

Our Father, and our God, we know that the foundations of the temple of Israel in days of old were laid under Thy divine guidance—that shouts of joy arose from the hearts of the people, and they praised Thee, because the foundation was laid. Hear our prayer, O God, and accept this work of our hands. Add to it Thy divine blessing. May we be stirred with joy and thanksgiving that the foundation of this house is laid. May our service today be well pleasing in Thy sight. Grant this, O Lord, our strength and our Redeemer. Amen.

The Doxology.

(Then the minister should read this selection of Scripture: Ezra 3:10-13.)

Hymn: "Faith of Our Fathers," or "I Love Thy Kingdom, Lord."

(Here a brief, appropriate address may be given, and/or greetings from other local ministers may be offered.)

(Deposits in the Corner Stone Chest may be presented by appropriate personnel at this moment, including—

A History of the Local Church
A Story of the Building Enterprise
A Membership Roll
A List of the Officers and Other Leaders of the Church
A Roll of Those listed in the Various Departments of the Church
A Picture of the Architect's Drawing of the Church Plant
A Bible
A Copy of the Corner Stone Laying Service)

Solo: "Bless This House"—Taylor-Brahe (with instrumental accompaniment).

Benediction: (Use the Aaronic benediction—Numbers 6:24-26).

NOTE: It is always the part of wisdom to use as many persons as possible in a service such as this. Have copies of the program printed in dignified form to lend significance to the occasion.

A CONSECRATION PRAYER SERVICE

(This form is suggested for use when the congregation meets in the new church for the first time, probably a Sunday or two before the dedication. The Service will begin in front of the church.)

"I have built Thee an exalted house, a place for Thee to dwell in for ever."
—II Chronicles 6:2.

CALL TO WORSHIP: Psalm 95:1-7 . . . . (Elder)

TRUMPET CALL TO WORSHIP:
"Holy, Holy, Holy" . . . . (Organist or Cornetist)

INVOCATION: . . . . (Elder)

HYMN: "'Tis the Blessed Hour of Prayer," or "To Thy Temple Holy"

SCRIPTURE LESSONS I Kings 8:22-30 . . . . (Deaconess)

PRESENTATION OF THE KEYS OF THE BUILDING—
   (Chairman of Plans and Construction)

For the architect and contractor, I present the keys of this building to the Building Council, assuring you that in design and workmanship it is worthy of the sacred use for which it is intended, a house of worship of the most high God.

ACCEPTANCE OF THE KEYS OF THE BUILDING—
   (Chairman of the Building Council)

As chairman of the Building Council, I receive these keys symbolizing our acceptance of this building erected under our direction for the congregation of this church, to be set apart from common uses to the worship of God, the preaching and teaching of the Gospel of Christ. I deliver to the Chairman of the Furnishings and Equipment Committee the keys to this edifice, symbolizing its readiness and the fulfillment of our commission.

PRESENTATION OF THE CHURCH BUILDING TO THE CON-
   GREGATION—(Chairman of the Furnishings and Equipment Committee)

As chairman of the Furnishings and Equipment Committee, I do now pass the keys of this church, constructed for the purpose of worship, fellowship, teaching, preaching, to the congregation of ....Church, to be used as the Church home of this congregation. I would urge everyone to exemplify in group and individual living the spirit of our Master, and to bear witness in this community to the mission and message of Christ whose name we delight to wear.

ACCEPTANCE OF THE CHURCH HOME OF............................
   (Chairman of the Church Board)

As chairman of the Official Board, I accept these keys. This congregation is conscious of the great responsibility which this acceptance places upon it, and is ready to covenant with God to hold this Church Home for the purpose in-

74

tended. I now present this building to our Minister to be consecrated to the Glory of God and His divine purposes.

Minister: We are indeed thankful that God has stirred the hearts of His people to provide this building and that He has prospered this undertaking. With gratitude we receive it for its intended use. Let us now proceed to set it apart to its proper and sacred uses, to the praise and honor of God and to the service of men in the loving spirit of Christ our Lord. Let us humbly unite our hearts in fervent prayer, thanking God for His goodness, and seeking His blessing.

People: We give thanks to Thee, O God; we give thanks; we call on Thy name and recount Thy wondrous deeds . . . Glorious art Thou, more majestic than the everlasting mountains.—Psalm 75:1; 76:4.

OPENING THE DOORS OF THE CHURCH . . . . (Caretaker)

(At this point the doors will be unlocked. The choir will move into the Church, led by the Minister and will proceed down the center aisle and into the Chancel. The people will follow, directed to their seats by the ushers. Organ music will be played.)

RESPONSIVE CALL TO WORSHIP . . . . (Elder)

LEADER: I was glad when they said to me, "let us go to the house of the Lord."

PEOPLE: Our feet have been standing within thy gates, O Jerusalem!

LEADER: One thing have I asked of the Lord, that will I seek after:

PEOPLE: That I may dwell in the House of the Lord all the days of my life, to behold the beauty of the Lord and to inquire in His Temple.

(Psalm 122:1, 2; 27:4)

LEADER: Unless the Lord builds the house, those who build it labor in vain.—Psalm 127:1.

HYMN: "Holy, Holy, Holy"

PRAYER: (Layman)—(Choral Response)

SPECIAL MUSIC (or Hymn): "Lord for Tomorrow and Its Needs"

THE LORD'S SUPPER

Minister: (John 3:16, 17)

Communion Hymn: "Have Thine Own Way" (2 stanzas)

(Prayers by Elders and Passing of Emblems)

OFFERING

Minister: Give, and it shall be given to you; good measure, pressed down, shaken together, running over, will he put into your lap. For the measure you give will be the measure you get back.— (Luke 6:38)

Offering is received

Doxology

Prayer of Dedication

ANTHEM: "God Is a Spirit" (or some other special number)

VOWS OF CONSECRATION . . . . (Led by an Elder)

We the members of .... Church pledge and covenant ourselves for Christ and the Church, for the Gospel and the Kingdom:

—To attend to the worship of God;

—To perpetuate a spiritual communion with Christ;

—To impart the Holy Spirit in our daily lives;

—To preach the Word;

—To support the work of the Church;

—To encourage each other by the spirit of cooperation;

—To look beyond the immediate community to world outreach of the Church;

—To pray for the peace of the world;

—To pray for the salvation of all men;

—To do all this and more for the sake of Christ. Amen.

PRAYER OF CONSECRATION . . . . (Minister)

RESPONSE: "The Lord's Prayer" by Malotte . . . . (Soloist)

INVITATION HYMN: "O Jesus, I Have Promised"

BENEDICTION: (Unison)

God, be merciful unto us, and bless us,
And cause his face to shine upon us;
That Thy way may be known upon the earth,
Thy salvation among all nations. Amen.

(Psalm 67:1, 2)

POSTLUDE by the Bells

A SUGGESTED SERIES OF DEDICATION SERVICES

(It is quite appropriate in these times, particularly
in the larger churches, to have a series of dedicatory services—a week of dedication—with prominent speakers, and with a different emphasis of
dedication each evening. The following may
serve as a sign-board to point the way.)

SUNDAY MORNING—

Dedication of the Sanctuary
Sermon: "The Supreme Purpose of the Church"

MONDAY NIGHT—

Community Night—Dedication of Fellowship Hall
(with dinner and dedication in Fellowship Hall)
Address: "The Tie of Christian Fellowship."

TUESDAY MORNING—

Annual Birthday Celebration and Dedication Services of Christian Women's Fellowship

Address: "The Life Abundant"

TUESDAY NIGHT—

Men's Banquet and Dedication Service of Christian Men's Fellowship

Address: "Rise Up, O Men of God"

WEDNESDAY NIGHT—

Youth Banquet and Dedication Service in Fellowship Hall

Address: "My Life a Channel of Blessing"

THURSDAY NIGHT—

Dedication of the Educational Building
(Worship in the Sanctuary)

Address: "The Church a School in Christian Living"

SUNDAY MORNING—

Dedication of the Church Building in Its Entirety

(Here may be included a Baptistry, the Pulpit Bible, the Pulpit, Windows, Communion Table, Library, and other significant portions of the building or furnishings.)

Sermon: "The Church in a Democracy"

SERVICE FOR THE DEDICATION
OF A CHURCH BUILDING

(A service of dedication requires thorough planning and great care in detail. This type of service should be "made to order" for the specific occasion in your church. In brief the program will generally take this form:)

1. Instrumental Prelude
2. Call to Worship, or Introit
3. Processional Hymn
4. Invocation and the Lord's Prayer
5. Choral Response
6. Scripture Reading
7. Special Music
8. Dedicatory Address
9. Offering
10. Doxology
11. Dedication by the Minister
12. Litany of Dedication
13. Dedicatory Anthem
14. Prayer of Dedication
15. Delivery of Keys, by Chairman of Building Committee to Trustees, with short statement by each
16. Congratulatory Remarks by Visiting Ministers
17. Benediction

—OR—

1. Organ Prelude
2. Hymn
3. Scripture Reading
4. Prayer of Thanksgiving
5. Solo: "Bless This House"—Taylor-Brahe
6. Delivery of Keys to Trustees, and Acceptance
7. Dedication Sermon
8. Contributions

9. Prayer of Dedication
10. Litany of Dedication (all standing and reading from a printed form)
11. Closing Hymn
12. Benediction

NOTE: In any event this should be a service of dignity. A brochure, or printed form should be used.

A LITANY OF DEDICATION

(This form or some adaptation of it may serve your purpose in a dedication of a church building. Build your own program and litany in keeping with your local situation:)

MINISTER: Under the providence of God we have come to this glad hour when the building our hearts have long desired has become a reality and is to be dedicated to its holy purpose. Let us humbly unite in prayer as we thank God for His goodness, and seek His blessing.

PEOPLE: Blessed art Thou, O Lord God, our Father. Wondrous things are accomplished through Thy power. We glorify Thy matchless name!

MINISTER: To the end that Christian worship may be central in the life of this congregation, we dedicate this Sanctuary to the adoration of God.

PEOPLE: God is spirit, and those who worship Him must worship in spirit and truth.

MINISTER: To the observance of the Lord's Supper, in memory of the boundless love of Christ, we dedicate this Table of Remembrance.

PEOPLE: Present your bodies as a living sacrifice, holy and acceptable to God which is your spiritual worship.

MINISTER: To the reading of the Holy Scriptures, and to the witness of the Open Bible, we dedicate this Lectern.

PEOPLE: Thy Word is a lamp to my feet, and a light to my path.

MINISTER: For the proclamation of the Good News of the Kingdom of God to all who enter this Sanctuary, we dedicate this Pulpit.

PEOPLE: Thy Kingdom come, Thy will be done, on earth as it is in heaven.

MINISTER: For those who come to receive the Christian Ordinance of Baptism as a token of obedience and a dedication of life, and who rise to walk in newness of life, we dedicate this Baptistry.

PEOPLE: We were buried therefore with Him by baptism into death, so that as Christ was raised from the dead by the glory of the Father, we too might walk in newness of life.

MINISTER: To Him who said, "I am the Light of the World," and for the sake of all to whom He said, "Ye are the Light of the World," we dedicate these Windows.

PEOPLE: For it is the God who said, "Let light shine out of darkness," who has shone in our hearts to give the light of the knowledge of the glory of God in the face of Christ.

MINISTER: For souls who may find peace and rest as they sing hymns, in prayer and meditation, even as the silent steeple rises to catch the first ray of dawn with its quiet dignity, we dedicate this lovely Edifice.

PEOPLE: Come to me, all who labor and are heavy laden and I will give you rest.

MINISTER: For little children who will be committeed to the loving care of the Heavenly Father, and for the youth who will be guided to the call of Christ, and for their parents who seek to know the highest affection, the noblest discipline, and the purest religion, we dedicate this House of God.

PEOPLE: And he said to him, "Follow Me," and he left everything, and rose and followed Him.

MINISTER: To the spirit of fruitful fellowship and Christian love in the life and work of the church, we dedicate this place of assembly.

PEOPLE: For as in one body we have many members . . . So we though many, are one body in Christ, and individually members one of another.

MINISTER: In grateful remembrance of those who have gone before us and for the blessed hope of a house not made with hands, eternal in the heavens; we dedicate this House of God.

PEOPLE: In my Father's house are many rooms, . . . I go to prepare a place for you.

MINISTER: That those who mourn may receive hope and comfort while walking through the dark valleys of life, we dedicate this Church.

PEOPLE: Let not your hearts be troubled; believe in God; believe also in me.

MINISTER: For those desiring God's Companionship at the very beginning of their wedded life, and come to the House of God to exchange their vows in His Presence, we dedicate this Shrine to Him who honored and blest the marriage in Cana of Galilee.

PEOPLE: Be subject to one another out of reverence for Christ.

MINISTER: To the unfinished task of World Friendship, we dedicate this Church House.

PEOPLE: You shall be my witnesses in Jerusalem and in all Judea and Samaria and to the end of the earth.

MINISTER: With sincere gratitude and heart-felt appreciation to all, who by their time, their talent, their treasure, their love and prayers have made this dream a reality.

ALL: *We dedicate this Christian Church.*

MINISTER: Let us unite in fervent prayer.

ALL: We consecrate to Thee, our Father, this building to be henceforth the Holy place of Thy presence with us, and the gateway to heaven. We set it apart from all common and worldly uses to be Thy Sanctuary, where Thy Word shall be proclaimed and taught, Thy Ordinances celebrated, where prayers shall be made unto Thee, and where Thy Mind and Spirit shall play upon ours. Let Thy Glory fill this House and dwell in it forevermore. Amen.

A PRAYER OF DEDICATION

Eternal Father God, the Source of all abiding truth, the Destiny of all worthy achieving, the Father of our Lord Jesus Christ, we come before Thee on this inspiring occasion with our hearts filled with gratitude.

Do Thou, O Father, accept the work of our hands expressed in this House of Prayer as we set it apart to Thy Word and work, and use it for the glory and honor of Thy name. May it be to us and to our children through all the coming years a shrine of blessed memories. May it be a refuge from the cares and anxieties and burdens of daily living—a place where we may gather strength and light from above. Make it a shelter from every distress. May we come to this hallowed place in faith that we may receive the benediction and peace of our Lord Jesus Christ. May this house be dedicated to the defense of Liberty of thought and speech in the Lord. May it be used for the Glory of God; for the broadcasting of His message of Life; for the advancement of the Heavenly Kingdom in which souls are redeemed and upbuilded in Christ.

As the erection of the temple is vain without the consecration of the people, we offer Thee our souls anew. Through Thy Word dwell in our hearts. May we here be changed into Thine image that we may reflect Thy love and glory. May Christ be formed in us that we may reflect Thy Gospel in the lives of others.

As we offer to Thee this place of assembly, this house that we have builded, do Thou receive it as we humbly dedicate it to Thee. We set it apart for Thy worship—for the offering of prayer and thanksgiving; for the sacrifice of broken and contrite hearts; for the reading, hearing, teaching of Thy Word; for the unfolding of Thy will for mankind; for the administering of the Christian Sacraments. May we prove by our lives that we are worthy stewards of Thy manifold grace. Come, O Lord, and make this house now and forever Thy dwelling place. Fill it with Thy glorious Presence. Upon wall and window, upon lintel and door-post, upon pulpit and pew, and organ, may there be written, Holiness to the Lord.

Our Father, bless those who minister here—may they be vessels fitted for the Master's use and as they pray to Thee for strength to do and to be, hear Thou in Thy celestial abode and bless their ministry abundantly as they seek to guide the souls of men in paths of righteousness. When tired, sin-sick, hungry hearts come here with their need, O hear Thou their appeal and grant that they may find the bread and water of life.

Hear our prayer and accept this house and use it to Thy glory. We pray in our Master's name. Amen.—E. L. YOUNG.

SERVICE OF DEDICATION
FOR THE SANCTUARY

(Persons may be seated during any period marked*)

ORGAN: "Grave and Allegro"
   from "2nd Sonata"................*Mendelssohn*
   (Your silence during this period will assist those who desire to begin this hour of worship with music and reverent meditation)

INTROIT

PROCESSIONAL: "For the Beauty of the Earth"
   (Standing, all stanzas)
   (The congregation will be seated at the close of the hymn)

*ORGAN INTERLUDE

CALL TO WORSHIP

MINISTER: O come, let us sing unto the Lord;
   Let us make a joyful noise unto the rock of our salvation.

PEOPLE: Let us come before His presence with thanksgiving.
   Let us make a joyful noise unto Him with psalms.

MINISTER: For the Lord is a great God,
   And a great king above all gods.

PEOPLE: O come, let us worship and bow down;
   Let us kneel before the Lord our maker.

CHORALE (Choir and Congregation)
   "O Thou by whom we come to God,
   The Life, the Truth, the Way,
   The path of prayer Thyself hast trod.
   Lord, teach us how to pray."

THE LORD'S PRAYER

THREE-FOLD AMEN ....Choir

*ORGAN INTERLUDE

READING OF THE SCRIPTURE

CALL TO PRAISE
> MINISTER: O Lord, open thou our lips.
> CHOIR: And our mouths shall show forth thy praise.
> MINISTER: Praise ye the Lord.
> CHOIR: The Lord's name be praised. Amen.

GLORIA PATRI (Standing)

*ORGAN INTERLUDE

CALL TO PRAYER
> MINISTER: The Lord be with you.
> PEOPLE: And with thy spirit.
> MINISTER: Let us pray.

"BLESS THE LORD"...............................Choir

PRAYER

SEVEN-FOLD AMEN...............................Choir

OFFERING SERVICE

ANTHEM: "Sanctus"...........................*Gounod*

DOXOLOGY

DEDICATION AND CHORAL RESPONSE

COMMUNION HYMN: "Here at Thy Table, Lord"
> (Stanzas 1 and 2)

THE LORD'S SUPPER
> This is a feast of remembrance and fellowship. Any
> who wish are invited to partake of the loaf and cup
> which are symbolic of the life and suffering of our
> Master, and which suggest a spiritual union with all
> His followers.

HYMN: "A Charge to Keep I Have" ....
> (Standing, Stanzas 1 and 2)

SERMON: "Torch, Book and Cross"

LITANY OF DEDICATION:

Longing for the increase of His Kingdom in the hearts of men everywhere; providing for our unending need to continue steadfastly in the Apostles' doctrine, in fellowship, in the breaking of bread and in prayers; desiring to offer to a growing community a House of Prayer that all who enter may find God "in the beauty of holiness"; we have builded this sanctuary and are now come for its dedication to the high calling of Christian Worship.

MINISTER: For the proclamation of the Good News to all who enter these portals:

PEOPLE: We dedicate this Thy House, O God.

MINISTER: For those restless, weary souls who may find their peace and rest as they rise toward God in the singing of hymns, in prayer and meditation, even as the great tower rises to catch the first ray of dawn with its peace and quiet;

PEOPLE: We dedicate this house of prayer to an ever listening God.

MINISTER: Toward the earnest search for Truth wherever found in the secrets of God's good earth, and above all, that Truth revealed in Holy Writ which puts Eternity in our hearts, and binds those who seek in a fruitful fellowship of life and work by His power that worketh in us;

PEOPLE: We dedicate this Temple to Him who is the source of Truth.

MINISTER: For the stranger who enters here and is caught up by the spirit of heart warming love within these hallowed walls and becomes one with the company of believers in worship as all hearts are blended in praise and thanksgiving;

PEOPLE: We dedicate this Haven, our Father.

MINISTER: For little children who will be committed to the loving care of the Heavenly Father, and their parents who seek to know the highest affection, the noblest discipline and the purest religion;

PEOPLE: We dedicate this blessed Church Home.

MINISTER: That those who mourn may receive hope and light and be comforted while walking through the dark valleys of life;

PEOPLE: We dedicate this Dwelling of His Spirit.

MINISTER: For those desiring God's companionship at the outset of their wedded life, and come to this Holy place to exchange their solemn vows in His Presence;

PEOPLE: We dedicate this Shrine to Him who blest the marriage at Cana.

MINISTER: For those who come to receive the Holy Rite of Baptism as a token of obedience and dedication and rise to walk in newness of life;

PEOPLE: We dedicate this place of life commitment.

MINISTER: For the sacred moments of Communion when the children of God, in penitence and humility, observe the Lord's Supper as a remembrance of His sacrificial death for our redemption, joining with all Christians about His Table, as one Family with one Faith and one Father;

PEOPLE: We dedicate this Blessed Sanctuary.

UNISON PRAYER: With grateful hearts and joyous spirits we lift our voices to give to Thee this work of our hands, this dream of our hearts. Grant to us who will serve and worship here the height and breadth, the grandeur and strength epitomized in this Temple which we dedicate to Thee. Sanctify, O God, both our coming in and

88

going forth. Enrich our lives through worship, and deepen in us our discipleship through service. Quicken in us the spirit of courage and confidence that we may go forth from here to fashion something good from all the experiences of each day.

Thine, O Lord is the greatness, and the power, and the glory and the victory, and the majesty, for all that is in the heaven and in the earth is Thine; Thine is the Kingdom, O Lord. Thou art exalted as head above all. Amen.

HYMN OF INVITATION AND CONSECRATION:
    "Blest Be the Tie That Binds"
        (Standing, all stanzas)

BENEDICTION

THE GIFT OF PEACE

POSTLUDE

A PRAYER OF DEDICATION

(For use on front cover of a dedication bulletin when a church sanctuary is to be dedicated.)

God, make the door of this house we have raised to Thee
Wide enough to receive all who need human love and fellow-
    ship and a Father's care;
Narrow enough to shut out all envy, pride and hate.
Make its threshold smooth enough to be no stumbling block
    to childish, weak or straying feet;
But rugged enough to turn back the Tempter's power.
God, make the door of this house
The gateway to Thy Eternal Kingdom.

                                    R. W. Jablonowski

SERVICE OF DEDICATION
THE CHAPEL OF THE GOOD SHEPHERD

PRELUDE: "The Lord is My Shepherd".........*Edmundson*

CALL TO WORSHIP

INVOCATION

HYMN: "Saviour, Like a Shepherd Lead Us"
(standing, all verses)

SCRIPTURE READING: John 10:1-18; Psalm 23

SPECIAL MUSIC: "The King of Love My Shepherd Is".*Shelley*

PRAYER

HYMN: "Shepherd of Souls, Refresh and Bless"
(standing, all verses)

AN APPRECIATION OF THE CHAPEL
OF THE GOOD SHEPHERD

SERMON
"Feeling after God to Find Him"

THE LITANY OF DEDICATION

MINISTER: Contemplating the use of the Chapel of the Good Shepherd for enriching moments of quiet meditation; for the uniting of life partners in the holy bonds of matrimony; for the ministry of comfort to those in the valley of sorrow; for the feeding of those in spiritual hunger; and the deepening of faith in those who live in fear of evil; we come to dedicate this shrine of worship to the Good Shepherd who knoweth his sheep by name.

To those healing moments of quiet reflection, when as his flock beside the still waters, we sense the presence of the Shepherd and acknowledge his boundless mercy.

PEOPLE: We prayerfully dedicate this Chapel.

MINISTER: That the sacred vows of love, uniting man and woman in holy matrimony may here be pledged in the presence of the Good Shepherd, and that His blessing upon the sacred venture may be reverently sought,

PEOPLE: We dedicate this Chapel.

MINISTER: That the ministry of comfort may be available to those who mourn, that those who walk through the valley of the shadow of death may fear no evil,

PEOPLE: We dedicate this Chapel to the Good Shepherd whose rod and staff are symbols of the Divine Protection, and whose love is our source of comfort.

MINISTER: As a shrine of penitence for those who have strayed from the paths of righteousness; who are burdened with a broken conscience and are seeking forgiveness; that here they may, by confession and repentance, lay their burden on the Saviour and be restored to the fold of the Shepherd who went into the mountain to find his lost sheep,

PEOPLE: We dedicate in deepest gratitude, this Chapel of the Seeking Shepherd, who giveth his life for his sheep.

MINISTER: To those occasions of great decision when the soul of youth is struggling between the high road and the low; that they may here discover the true perspective, and choose the Unseen and Eternal,

PEOPLE: We trustingly dedicate this Chapel of the Good Shepherd, who himself was once the youth of Nazareth and learned obedience by the things he suffered.

MINISTER: In recognition of our fellowship with all other Christians of every race and creed; and striving for The One Great Church of Christ who said, Other sheep have I that are not of this fold,

PEOPLE: We dedicate this Chapel that there may be one fold, one shepherd.

MINISTER: In grateful prayer for those whose love has provided this holy place, and in the blessed memory of Elizabeth Tevis Herd,

PEOPLE: We fervently unite in the solemn dedication of this Chapel of the Good Shepherd; and in His holy presence rededicate our lives to Him; that goodness and mercy may follow us all the days of our lives and that we may dwell in the House of the Lord forever. Amen.

PRAYER OF DEDICATION........................Minister

HYMN: "O Thou Whose Own Vast Temple Stands"

(standing)

BENEDICTION

POSTLUDE

A LITANY OF DEDICATION

(An alternate Litany Of Dedication for use in dedicating an Education Building and Fellowship Hall. The ritual leading up to this litany would include prelude, call to worship, invocation, hymn, responsive reading, solo, prayer, offering, doxology, introduction of visiting speaker, hymn, address of dedication.)

THE LITANY OF DEDICATION:

MINISTER: In recognition of the Great Commission which bids us "Go—make disciples—baptize—teach," and in harmony with the message which reads that "Jesus advanced in wisdom, in stature, and in favor with God and man" we come to this moment of dedication praying that blessings in over-flowing abundance may prevail in the hearts of all who have made this happy moment possible.

To the sowing of the good seed of the Kingdom in the hearts of all of our people, young and old,

PEOPLE: We dedicate our Education Building to the ministry of teaching.

MINISTER: To the purpose of developing a school where the Holy Scriptures may be read, interpreted, and known,

PEOPLE: We dedicate our Education Building.

MINISTER: For the spiritual enrichment of life as it unfolds through childhood,

PEOPLE: We dedicate our building.

MINISTER: For the nurture of youth and the enrichment of the home,

PEOPLE: We dedicate our building.

MINISTER: To provide an appointed place where the soul of man may quest for the Good, the Beautiful and the True,

PEOPLE: We dedicate our building.

MINISTER: To make accessible an atmosphere where the art of worship may be rehearsed and learned,

PEOPLE: We dedicate our building.

MINISTER: For the training of life in the Christian Way, that character may reflect the life of the Master,

PEOPLE: We dedicate our building.

MINISTER: To maintain a school of intelligent faith, wherein we may learn to give a reason for the faith that is in us,

PEOPLE: We dedicate our building.

MINISTER: For the enrichment of social and recreational life through fellowship with those who share in the mind of Christ,

PEOPLE: We dedicate our Education and Fellowship Building.

MINISTER AND PEOPLE: We now, the people of this church and congregation, compassed about with a great cloud of witnesses, remembering the sacrifices of the fathers, upon whose foundations we are building, dedicate ourselves anew to the teaching of the word of God in both precept and example.
Bless the Lord, O my soul;
And all that is within me, bless His holy name. Amen.

PRAYER OF DEDICATION

BENEDICTION

POSTLUDE

FORM FOR A CHURCH DEDICATION ANNIVERSARY

(This service was used on the fortieth anniversary
of the Dedication of a Church Building. It is quite
simple and direct.)

PRELUDE .... Pianist

CALL TO WORSHIP: (In unison)
> One thing have I asked of the Lord,
> that will I seek after;
> That I may dwell in the house of the
> Lord all the days of my life,
> To behold the beauty of the Lord, and
> to inquire in His temple.
> —Psalm 27:4.

HYMN: "God of Grace and God of Glory"—(Standing)

INVOCATION AND THE LORD'S PRAYER

SCRIPTURE READING: Psalms 133 and 150

PRAYER HYMN: "O God, Thy World is Sweet with Prayer"
(One stanza)

THE PASTORAL PRAYER

OFFERING SERVICE
> Sentence of Scripture
> The Offertory
> Doxology
> Prayer of Dedication

COMMUNION SERVICE
> Hymn: "Here at Thy Table, Lord", (1, 2)
> The Lord's Supper
> Hymn: "Here at Thy Table, Lord", (3)

AN AFFIRMATION OF FAITH: (In Unison)

> I believe in God,
>> Creator and Sustainer of the universe
>>> —My Father.
>
> I believe in Jesus Christ,
>> The Way, the Truth, and the Life
>>> —My Saviour.
>
> I believe in Man,
>> His ideals, his aspirations and dreams
>>> —My Brother.
>
> I believe in Myself,
>> What I am, what I hope to be, and what,
>> by God's grace, I shall be.
>>> —My Best Self.
>
>> *—Rudolph Charles Tatsch.*

SOLO: "Bless This House".................*Taylor-Brahe*

SERMON: "Except the Lord Build the House

HYMN OF INVITATION AND CONSECRATION

HYMN: "O Master Let Me Walk With Thee" (tune, Maryton)

RESPONSE OF DEDICATION

MINISTER: In the spirit of gratitude to our Heavenly Father, by whose favor, inspiration and guidance we have come to this, the Fortieth Anniversary of the Dedication of this Church Building—

CONGREGATION: We re-dedicate this House of Worship.

MINISTER: In love for our Church Home and in reverent memory of all those who by their sacrificial gifts down through the years have bequeathed to us this valuable Church property—

CONGREGATION: We re-dedicate this House of Worship.

MINISTER: In grateful appreciation of the faithfulness of friends and members of this congregation, the prevailing spirit of unity and loyalty throughout the congregation and community—

CONGREGATION: We re-dedicate this House of God today, and re-consecrate our lives to the service of Christ our Lord, and to the world-outreach of His Kingdom.

BENEDICTION

"THREE-FOLD AMEN"

POSTLUDE

FORM OF PIPE ORGAN DEDICATION SERVICE

PRELUDE: "Adagio" from Sonata in C . . . . *Guilmant*

PROCESSIONAL HYMN:

> "God of Our Fathers, Whose Almighty Hand"
>> (Congregation will rise and sing with the choir)

CALL TO WORSHIP: (Minister)
> Make a joyful noise to God, all the earth;
> Sing the glory of his name;
> Give to him glorious praise . . .
> All the earth worships thee;
> They sing praises to thee,
> Sing praises to thy name.

> > > > > —Psalm 66:1, 2, 4.

GLORIA PATRI: (standing)

THE LORD'S PRAYER: (seated)

ANTHEM: "O Lord Most Merciful" . . . . *Concone*

RESPONSIVE SCRIPTURE READING: Psalm 67

PRAYER: (Minister)

OFFERTORY: "Jesu, Joy of Man's Desiring" . . . . *Bach*
> Prayer of Dedication
> Doxology

THE LORD'S SUPPER
> Communion Hymn: "Bread of the World in Mercy Broken"
> Meditation and Words of Institution
> Communion: (All followers of Christ are invited to partake)

A WORD REGARDING THE ORGAN: (By Choir Director)

(This statement should cover such items as source,
make, possibilities, gratitude for all who have
contributed, a word of commendation to organist.)

ANTHEM: "Sanctus" .... *Gounod*

A STATEMENT OF DEDICATION: (By Minister)

LITANY OF DEDICATION

MINISTER: Father of our Lord Jesus Christ: our Father who
art in heaven: in whom we live and move and have
our being—

PEOPLE: To Thee we dedicate this organ.

MINISTER: Son of God, our Lord and Saviour and Advo-
cate with the Father, Head of the body which is the
church: Prophet, Priest, and King of thy people: Wonderful Counsellor, Mighty God, Everlasting Father,
Prince of Peace—

PEOPLE: To Thee we dedicate this organ.

MINISTER: Holy Spirit of God, given to be our Helper,
Guide and Comforter: Lord and Giver of life—

PEOPLE: To Thee we dedicate this organ.

MINISTER: We pray that all troubled hearts and minds
who here seek healing, comfort, inspiration and rest
may find in this instrument a source of great helpfulness.

PEOPLE: For this purpose we dedicate this organ.

MINISTER: For the leading and inspiring of service in
song, that all people may praise the Lord—

PEOPLE: We dedicate this organ.

UNISON: For the glory of God and the service of man we would dedicate our lives and yield ourselves constantly unto his will, so that each day and hour we may be in tune with his Infinite Spirit. In the joy of our Lord Christ we dedicate this organ to the worship of God immortal, in whom all harmonies are one, who made us so that in music we can hear His voice; to Christ, our Saviour, Friend and Master, we dedicate ourselves for the advancement of His Kingdom in the hearts and lives of men. To Him be praise and glory in the Eternal Spirit, world without end.

PRAYER OF DEDICATION

HYMN: "Joyful, Joyful, We Adore Thee"

BENEDICTION

POSTLUDE: "Largo and Finale"............. *Wolstenholme*

FORM FOR DEDICATION OF
CHURCH FURNISHINGS

(The specific items of church furnishings to be dedicated will be included. The following service was actually used in one church. Appropriate items may be added to or taken from the wording of the litany of dedication.)

PRELUDE: "Great Is Thy Faithfulness"............*Runyan*
(Tune—"Faithfulness")

CALL TO WORSHIP

MINISTER: The Lord is in His holy temple; let all the earth keep silence before him.

PEOPLE: Surely the Lord is in this place. This is none other than the house of God, and this is the gate of heaven.

MINISTER: O come, let us worship and bow down; Let us kneel before the Lord our Maker.

PEOPLE: For he is our God; and we are the people of his pasture and the sheep of his hand.

—Habbakuk 2:20; Psalm 95; Genesis 28:16, 17

INVOCATION

HYMN: "Lord, We Come Before Thee Now"

SCRIPTURE READING: Psalm 118:22-29

STATEMENT OF THE PURPOSE OF THIS ASSEMBLY

PRESENTATION OF THE ITEMS TO BE DEDICATED

ACCEPTANCE OF THE ITEMS FOR DEDICATION

SOLO: "Bless This House"................*Taylor-Brahe*

LITANY OF DEDICATION

MINISTER: To Thee, Our Father, we bring these tokens of loving service, and symbols of our Christian Faith that our lives may be enriched and our worship strengthened through their use.

PEOPLE: Hear, O Lord, our humble prayer of dedication.

MINISTER: To the glory of God and the telling of the gospel story to all who pass by,

PEOPLE: We dedicate the sign which beckons each passerby to come within and worship.

MINISTER: To the uplifting of our hearts in the singing of hymns and making melody in our hearts,

PEOPLE: We dedicate this piano.

MINISTER: To the fellowship of kindred minds gathered at the Table of Thy Presence.

PEOPLE: We dedicate this Communion Table in thoughtful reverence.

MINISTER: To the growing appreciation of the appropraite symbols of our faith—the cross on which our Saviour gave His life, the candles which tell of the divine and human elements of our worship, and the vases which contain the beauties of Thy wonderful world,

PEOPLE: We dedicate these symbols of faith, hope, love and beauty.

MINISTER: To the truth of the gospel as revealed in art, in color, in beautiful design,

PEOPLE: We dedicate this stained glass window.

MINISTER: To the preaching and the teaching of the Word of Truth through the Bible and from the pulpit,

PEOPLE: We dedicate this pulpit, and this Holy Bible resting upon it.

MINISTER: And now, our Father, to the enriching of our Christian experiences and the enlarging of our worship in Thy house where prayer is wont to be made,

PEOPLE: We dedicate these earthly symbols to their rightful uses in lifting the aspirations of this and future generations, that in this house of worship Thy name may be praised and Thy service glorified. Amen.

HYMN OF DEDICATION:

"When the Heart with Joy O'erflowing"

BENEDICTION

NOTE: If possible have several visiting ministers participate in this service.

SUGGESTIONS FOR USE IN
DEDICATING A HOME

(Significant observance of Christian Family week often includes the dedication of a home. Such a service should be simple, informal and warm-hearted. It should provide for natural participation of every member of the family as far as possible, and preferably should include only the family group and a few intimate friends.)

A PRELIMINARY STATEMENT: (The Minister)

Homemakers young and old are growing in appreciation of home life, and, children and youth are ready to respond when given opportunity.

Although other agencies can perform functions once held more closely within the family group, the home still remains the hallowed spot where understanding, love, and mutual respect are shared most satisfactorily. In the providence of God it is planned that way. The most wholesome security is that found in the Christian home.

Beyond a doubt the Festival of the Christian Home, or some similar recognition of family life is growing in favor. We are together here in this home this evening to hold a simple service of dedication. All of us will share in it. May God bless this home!

SCRIPTURE READING FROM THE FAMILY BIBLE:

A Home Jesus Visited: Luke 10:38-42.

Good Home Atmosphere: I John 4:7-21.

A Home-maker's Prayer

O Lord of Lovers, Shepherd of Adoring Hearts,

I thank thee for one who is lovelier than a Madonna lily,
rising whitely above blue larkspur . . .

Give us a home within the weathered walls of an ancient
house . . . a house made holy by the aspirations of the
revered dead . . .

Fill our home with quietness, adorn its walls with beauty,
and may love carry the key to every door . . .

May the stars swing low above our humble roof,

May the punctual whip-poor-will serenade us when the
year is young.

If we must suffer, go hungry, and grow old, may our days
be as glorious as autumn fruit . . .

If we must lose the zest of spring, may our love be as
everlasting as the ancient pines . . .

Give us the wealth which cannot be squandered in the
marketplace . . .

Give us abiding companionship, infinite comprehension,
and a trust which laughs at boastful death.

Amen.

—Harry Elmore Hurd

Hymn: "All Things Are Thine; No Gift Have We"

Candle-Lighting Ceremony—Symbol of Home Cheer

(While one lights candles, another says:)

There are many lights of home but love that goes from
heart to heart is the brightest of all.

(When the candles have been lighted, someone continues:)

Love is an incense from an altar bright
Where candles shine with clear and mellow light;
It is a lamp that cheers us when we roam,
And a kindly spark that lights the fires of home.

LIGHTING THE HEARTH-FIRE—SYMBOL OF HOSPITALITY

(If there is a fireplace let the husband put on kindling and light the fire, the wife reading:)

> "Kneel always when you light a fire
> Kneel reverently
> To God for his unfailing charity."
>
> —John Oxenham.

(Others may add sticks or twigs.)

AN AFFIRMATION

We who make up this family believe that we have been united by a power higher than ourselves. Controlled by the spirit of love we desire that every plan and act, every thought and word shall be worthy of the love which we have expressed, and that disagreements which come may be resolved in the spirit of fairness and affection.

ACT OF DEDICATION

Husband: We dedicate this house with appreciation of its builders and with gratitude for God's leading which has brought us here to make a home.

Wife: We dedicate the doors to security and to hospitality.

Husband: We dedicate the windows as receivers of light, and as means of looking out with kindness toward other homes.

Wife: We dedicate our furniture and equipment with pleasant thoughts of all those whose work adds to our comfort.

Husband: We dedicate our books as invitations to fellowship with great souls, and as bearers of the truth that makes us free.

Wife: We dedicate our pictures as symbols of all things beautiful.

Husband: We dedicate this home to work and leisure, to serious thought and the gaiety of laughter, to music and the lifting of the heart.

Wife: We dedicate this home to love and comradeship, to courage and patience, to courtesy and mutual understanding, to loyalty and high fellowship.

Husband: We dedicate the life of this home to the service of God and man as a unit of the Kingdom of God and a threshold to the life eternal.

PRAYER OF DEDICATION: (The Minister)

HYMNS AND SONGS OF GOOD FELLOWSHIP

(Sing some of the old favorite hymns, folk-songs, spirituals, and others.)

CLOSING PRAYER

The Lord bless us and keep us,

The Lord make his face to shine upon us, and be gracious unto us.

The Lord lift up His countenance upon us, and give us peace. Amen.

A PARSONAGE DEDICATION SERVICE

(Significant attention is being given these days to the Christian Family. At the dedication of a Parsonage, opportunity is offered to acquaint the congregation with the minister's home and family, and, at the same time to suggest that other homes may be dedicated, particularly homes of young couples who are just beginning their family. The following service of home dedication was used at an evening hour on the lawn of the parsonage.)

MALE QUARTET: "I Want My Life
to Tell for Jesus".........................*Lorenz*

CALL TO WORSHIP: Isaiah 55:6,7 (Minister)

HYMN OF PRAISE: "For the Beauty of the Earth"

INVOCATION: (A visiting minister)

SCRIPTURE READING: Matthew 7:24-27 (Another visiting minister)

PRESENTATION OF KEYS: (Chairman of the Building Committee)

ACCEPTANCE OF KEYS: (Minister)

DOXOLOGY: (All standing)

MESSAGE: "The Home, God's First and Holiest School" (A mother)

MALE QUARTET: "Faith of Our Fathers"............*Hemy*
or
"Wonderful Story of Love"..........*Driver*

MINISTER: In the beginning God created the earth and all that in it is, clothed it with beauty and declared it to be good. This day we see this location and the house we have builded thereon as His creation, even as we are His, and the families that shall dwell therein are His. Therefore, that we may see and remember the beauty of His holiness, and that we are created in His image, we gratefully come to dedicate this lovely home.

PEOPLE: We dedicate these grounds and the home that stands upon them.

MINISTER: As these walls encircle and shelter those who shall dwell within them, may they forever be a symbol and reminder of God's encircling protection of our lives.

PEOPLE: We dedicate these walls.

MINISTER: That the door may be a reminder of Him who said, "I am the door," and added, "Come unto me," may all who enter here find understanding, rest and confidence, and go forth as messengers of Peace.

PEOPLE: We dedicate the door to this home.

MINISTER: That these windows may be symbols of the windows of the soul; open daily to receive the light of God's Spirit, and forever open the eyes of those who live here to new visions of service in the Kingdom of God.

PEOPLE: We dedicate these windows.

MINISTER: That those who dwell herein and those who find hospitality beneath the roof of this home,

PEOPLE: We dedicate the sheltering roof.

MINISTER: To the end that those who dwell within may ever feed upon the Word of God, and share the companionship of each other in calm assurance and love,

PEOPLE: We dedicate the rooms of this home.

MINISTER: That this house being set apart today may be a beacon light of Christian home life in this community and maintain a constant interest in the larger family of God.

PEOPLE: We do hereby dedicate this house in all its meaning to the service of God, knowing full well that "it takes a heap o' livin' in a house to make it a home," and that the Church of Jesus Christ is builded upon the family relationship which we today recognize.

PRAYER OF CONSECRATION: (A visiting minister)

CLOSING HYMN: "Lord, At This Closing Hour"......*Mason*

BENEDICTION: (An Elder)

RECEPTION WITHIN THE NEW PARSONAGE: (Minister and family to head the receiving line)

A SERVICE OF YOUTH DEDICATION

ORGAN MUSIC

HYMN: "Now in the Days of Youth"
    (Seated at close of hymn)
    (Standing)

RESPONSIVE READING: (Selections from I Timothy 4; Mark 10; II Timothy 2)

PRAYER HYMN: "Have Thine Own Way" (Stanzas 1 and 2)

EVENING PRAYER

PRAYER HYMN: "Have Thine Own Way" (Stanzas 3 and 4)

SOLO: "My Task" . . . . *Ashford*

MESSAGE: "Doing the Impossible"

LITANY OF DEDICATION:

> LEADER: To the end that every growing experience of the days of our youth may be an expression of Thy will being done on earth;
>
> That our friends, homes, school, church, nation and world may be touched by Thy hand working in us.
>
> PEOPLE: We dedicate ourselves to the principles and ideals of Jesus the Christ.
>
> LEADER: That the energy which quickens the muscles and nerves of our bodies may move to the defense of all that is good;
>
> That the skill and toil of our hands may create new beauty and usefulness for all men;
>
> That the capacity for new life divinely granted may ever be a sharing of Thy eternal continuation of the human race.

PEOPLE: We dedicate our physical selves with their sensations of strength, weariness, pleasure and pain to Thy work and toil among our fellow men.

LEADER: In the hope that our searching and study may reveal more of Thee and may present to us insights for the betterment of every nation;
With the conviction that contemplation of the past and present may guide us in making troublesome decisions in accordance with Thy will;
Desiring to exercise our reason that prejudice and ignorance may vanish;
In trust that our imaginations may form plans for self, home, and community upon Thy foundations.

PEOPLE: We give Thee our mental selves with their powers of thinking, reasoning, studying, and planning.

LEADER: That our sweeping emotions which carry us to love and hate alike may bring us only to love of all men;
That our binding friendships may unite young lives in a spirit of sharing;
That we may aspire to the high goals of life;
That our hearts may be filled with compassion for the oppressed of the world, moving our hands to acts of service.

PEOPLE: We dedicate our emotional selves with their compassion and anger, distress and happiness to Thine eternal and universal love and mercy.

LEADER: Searching after the purpose of life as a standard by which all else may be judged;
Desiring greatly to commune with Thee that we may know Thy will for us and for all men;
Praying that the spirit of Jesus the Christ may pervade our own spirits.

111

PEOPLE: We give unto Thee our spiritual selves which can be fed only by Thy Spirit, and strengthened only as we come unto Thee.

LEADER: Desiring that our hands may be Thy hands; that our thoughts may be of whatever is true, honorable, just, pure, lovely, excellent, and worthy of praise; Knowing that the greatest of all things is love; and that we must worship Thee in spirit and in truth.

PEOPLE: We hereby dedicate ourselves in obedience to the commandment of Jesus the Christ that "You shall love the Lord your God with all your heart and with all your soul, and with all your strength, and with all your mind; and your neighbor as yourself."

BENEDICTION

POSTLUDE

A SERVICE OF CONSECRATION

(For use as the closing of a State Youth Convention. May be adapted for other uses.)

THEME: "Renewal of Fellowship"

Aim: To direct the delegates in remembering the deep significance of their baptism into Christ, and to re-affirm their vows of loyalty to Him through dedication of life.

PRELUDE: "Traumerei".........................*S. Purcell*

HYMNIC CALL TO WORSHIP: "O Master, Let Me Walk with Thee" (first stanza—all singing)

INVOCATION: Almighty God, Lamp of our feet, whereby we trace our path, renew our spirits and draw our hearts unto Thee. Lift us above self-love, and the evil of our day, into the broad sunlight of Thy love, to live as those who have put on Christ. In His name. Amen.

RESPONSIVE SCRIPTURE READING: (Selections from Colossians 3 and II Corinthians 5—print the Scripture in your bulletin)

PRAYER HYMN: "Draw Thou My Soul, O Christ" (stanza 1)

A PERIOD OF GUIDED SILENT PRAYER

DEVOTIONAL TALKS "Returning With Power"—Luke 4:14

POEM OF ASPIRATION: "O Jesus, Youth of Nazareth"

(No. 217 in Christian Worship. Read it in unison.)

"These days together have meant much to each of us. We have been challenged; we have gained new heights of spiritual achievement. Our being here has been a distinct blessing—an unforgetable experience. Even this sanctuary, which has been the scene of many gatherings of significance, has become a hallowed place. Jesus, too, knew many sacred spots, places that had become meaningful because incidents, friendships, homes, great occasions—His talking with the doctors in the Temple, His first miracle in Cana of Galilee, His baptism by John at the Jordan. We know that it was at His baptism that Jesus dedicated His life to the Kingdom of God. It was then that He became more fully aware of His mission and of God's power and leading. We know that He chose the path of sacrifice and that He held steadily to this purpose under the will of God.

"Then, according to the story we read in Luke, 'Jesus returned in power of the Spirit into Galilee'—triumphant and victorious. He had dedicated Himself! We, too, can today adopt the way of sturdy heroism and in deed and truth say 'O Jesus, Thy Paths, Our Chosen Way'."

HYMN OF DEDICATION AND CONSECRATION: "Take My

Life, and Let It Be"
(Print the words in the bulletin)

114

Act of Dedication:

(Beginning with the persons in the section to the left, facing the pulpit, the delegates will rise and move in single file to the chancel. Before mounting the platform, each person will be handed a gummed cross; proceeding to the baptistry and the map of our State, he will place the cross on the map in an area approximately in the vicinity of the city from which he has come. He will then move off the platform and take a standing position by the wall of the sanctuary. At a signal by the leader, each one will cross his arms and clasp hands with those standing to the right and to the left, thus forming an endless chain. While in this position all will sing)—

Hymn: "O Jesus, I Have Promised" (stanza 1)

Benediction: (unison)

"God be merciful unto us, and bless us,
And cause His face to shine upon us;
That Thy way may be known upon the earth,
Thy salvation among all nations."

—Psalm 67:1,2

Note: One stanza of "God Be With You 'Til We Meet Again" or, "Into My Heart," may be used for the closing hymn. A Litany of Dedication may be worked out according to your own desire, based on I Corinthians 13, for use within this service.

A SERVICE OF WORSHIP AND DEDICATION

(For use on Woman's Day)

PRELUDE: "Andante Cantabile" from Symphony
No. 4 . . . . *Widor*

SILENT MEDITATION

HYMN: "When Thy Heart with Joy O'erflowing"
(Standing—all stanzas)

READING OF SCRIPTURE: Romans 12:1-21

MORNING PRAYER

SOLO: "Ave Maria" . . . . *Bach-Gounod*

OFFERTORY: "Our Father in Heaven" . . . . *Mendelssohn*

DEDICATION OF OFFERING

ADDRESS: "Women Serving Through Christ"

THE LITANY OF DEDICATION:

LEADER: For the inflowing of Thy divine love, which will
make our lives ever the unveiling of Thyself; our experiences a revelation of Thy ways among the children of men; our minds sanctuaries of Thy lowly
spirit which takes the common things of life and
makes them beautiful because Thou has written eternity upon them.

WOMEN: We join in humble prayer and joyous thanksgiving.

LEADER: That we may every day wisely use and gener-
ously share our unmerited blessings "that Thy way
may be known upon the earth" and in so doing jus-
tify every noble heritage, every worthy trust and every
gift of Thy love.

WOMEN: We pledge to so grow in the grace and knowledge of our Lord and Saviour, Jesus Christ.

LEADER: For the compelling desire in our hearts to identify ourselves with the Christian womanhood of the world whose sensitive heart of love and concern can reflect in our day and in our world the mind and spirit of Christ,

WOMEN: We make our supplication to an ever listening, patient Father, God.

LEADER: To become guardians of the home who shall in all circumstances practice those virtues of love which understand, forgive; are patient, serene, and unselfish; so that our family living may be rich in religious experience, equipping each member for all the demands of life,

WOMEN: With the assurance of Thy help we give ourselves.

LEADER: With consecration to these high purposes of our Christian faith, and confident that we may grow above the shallow, the unimportant, and the trivial to find for ourselves the significance, the sanctity and the nobility of life, to the glory of Christ and his Church,

WOMEN: We dedicate God's greatest gift, our lives.

THE PRAYER OF DEDICATION

BENEDICTION

A DEDICATION SERVICE FOR MEN

PRELUDE: "Largo"

PROCESSIONAL HYMN: "Forward Through the Ages"
(Congregation will stand and participate in the singing as the leaders enter.)

INVOCATION AND THE LORD'S PRAYER:
(Led by State Director CMF)

RESPONSIVE SCRIPTURE READING:
(Selections from Mark 1, John 18, Matthew 13—No. 11, "Christian Worship, A Hymnal")

PRAYER HYMN: "Dear Lord and Father of Mankind"

(Stanzas 1 and 5)

A PERIOD OF SILENCE FOR PRAYER AND MEDITATION

SOLO, OR MALE QUARTET:
"I Want My Life To Tell for Jesus".... *Breck-Lorenz*

MESSAGE: "Dedicated Men in Action"......... (Minister)

LITANY OF DEDICATION: (Led by District Governor CMF)

LEADER: In the train of the Man of Galilee who was God's example of the mastery of life, and who calls us to come up ever higher in personal purity and to strive toward perfection, as our Father in Heaven is perfect,

MEN: We yield our wills to His will and pray for power to follow in His footsteps.

LEADER: In the spirit of the Carpenter of Nazareth who was of good report in every affair of business and who brought dignity to honest toil by devoting its rewards to God and a nobler life,

MEN: We take as ours His dream of the Kingdom of God on earth, in our work and in our worship.

118

LEADER: In the faith of Him who drew a circle embracing all men and nations as the children of God, and who prayed that all might be one, to the end that the world may believe,

MEN: We pledge our loyalty to a church without class or human creed, as spacious as life and love, one church for the whole World.

HYMN OF DEDICATION: "Rise Up, O Men of God."
(Standing—sing all four stanzas)

BENEDICTION: (Unison)

Now unto Him who is able to do exceeding abundantly above all that we ask or think, according to the power that worketh in us, unto him be the glory in the Church and in Christ Jesus unto all generations for ever and ever. Amen.
—Ephesians 3:20.

NOTE: This Dedication Service for Men may be used as a part of a series of dedications of church personnel, or by adjustment it might serve the purpose of dedication of new officers, or a special group of men being set aside for a budget-raising campaign.

AN ORDER OF SERVICE FOR THE DEDICATION OF PARENTS AND CHILD

(This may very acceptably be called "The Blessing of a Little Child.")

Every child is born of God, hence it is of utmost importance to recognize the sacredness of birth and personality by a public service of dedication, or blessing, of parents and child. This service is not to be regarded as a sacrament nor as an ordinance, but rather as a significant religious ceremony lifted to the Nth degree in the life of the home and the church. The child is from God and belongs to God. The dedication of parents seeks to point up their sacred responsibility, and is designed to give paramount significance to the task of guidance and protection in behalf of the child in the home and in the church. Certainly this is fundamental. The blessing of little children was a common experience in the life of Jesus the Master Teacher. We would do well to follow His example.

The following copy of the Service for the Blessing of Little Children follows the essential content of the printed form referred to above.

A Form of Service for
THE BLESSING OF LITTLE CHILDREN
The Minister shall read:

"They brought young children to Christ, that he should touch them; and his disciples rebuked those that brought them. But when Jesus saw it, he was much displeased, and said unto them, Suffer the little children to come unto me, and forbid them not; for of such is the Kingdom of God. Verily I say unto you, Whosoever shall not receive the Kingdom of God as a little child, he shall not enter therein. And he took them up in his arms, put his hands upon them, and blessed them."—Mark 10:13-16.

The Minister shall say:

Dearly beloved, the divine-human task of developing a personality after the birth of a Child is the most delicate and serious work to which man is called. All the sights and sounds that play upon the sensitive little body help to determine his future characteristics. The love of the home affects the Child in a thousand ways for good. As the Child grows he may receive the spiritual life of his parents as a rose drinks in the sunlight. The religious conversation of a mother with her Child, even at a very tender age, will make for his fuller and richer growth. God will have access to your Child if you will keep the doors of your own lives open to Him. If the Child does not absorb the beautiful sense of God during the first critical period of the development of his personality, usually he will find the sense of God dim when he is grown up, and much more difficult to acquire.

Religion is natural to the human heart, and is, therefore, as much a part of the Child's nature as are his dependence on his parents and his trust in them. It is your duty, therefore, to receive this Child from God's hand and to teach *him* to know and love God, and, working in obedience to God's will to help in the unfolding of the Child's spiritual life. From your example the Child must learn to pray. From your example *he* must learn to read and love the Bible, and from your example *he* must learn the way of fellowship with Christ.

Above all you are to make it your constant prayer and effort to lead the Child to know and love Christ so that when *he* comes to the age of proper understanding *he* will choose of *his* own will to confess Christ as *his* Saviour, to obey Him, and to give *himself* in loyal and loving service as a member of the Church, which is the Body of Christ.

Then the Minister shall ask the parents the following questions:

Do you, Mr. and Mrs. . . . .
promise to pray for and with this Child for *his* growth in knowledge of God, and in the spiritual life?

The parents shall answer:

We do.

Do you promise to train this Child in body, mind, and soul for service to and fellowship with God?

The parents shall answer:

We do.

121

Do you promise to do all you can to lead *him* at the proper age to confess *his* faith in Christ?

The parents shall answer:

We do.

What is the name of this Child

The parents shall answer:

The name of this Child is.........................

Then the Minister shall say:

The name of this Child is.........................

Then the Minister shall say:

Let us pray.

O Lord, gracious and merciful, grant us Thy blessing as we wait before Thee. Teach these, Thy servants, the sacredness of parenthood, and the beauty of home life. Help them to see in this Child an opportunity from Thee, and help them so to walk before Thee that these tender feet may find the path of faith, truth, justice, honour, and righteousness. Give them patience, wisdom, judgment and heavenly favour in their task. Bless this Child O Lord, with strength of body, mind, and soul; and grant that the growth of this Child may ever be toward Thee; through Jesus Christ our Lord. Amen.

Then the Minister shall pronounce the Blessing:

The Lord bless thee, and keep thee;

The Lord make His face shine upon thee, and be gracious unto thee;

The Lord lift up His countenance upon thee and give thee peace;

Both now and in the life everlasting. Amen.

FORM FOR THE DEDICATION
OF A FUNERAL HOME

(This service should be printed and distributed to all in attendance.)

PRELUDE: (To be selected) . . . . Organ

CALL TO WORSHIP: (By presiding minister, rabbi or priest)

HYMN: "O God, Our Help in Ages Past" (stanzas 1 and 3. Print words in bulletin.)

INVOCATION: (By some appropriate clergyman)

STATEMENT BY THE OWNER AND MANAGER
OF THE FUNERAL HOME:

It is the sincere desire of this establishment to render a distinct and significant service in this community. Death comes to every one of us. We propose to serve in the hour of bereavement in the spirit of helpfulness, sharing our facilities, our skills, our services in such a way as to be reasonable, cooperative, friendly, comforting. In the hour of grief we are brought very close to one another in our religious moorings. May we always keep uppermost in our dealings the spirit of pure and undefiled religion.

A TRIBUTE OF PRAISE: (In recognition of the business enterprise and community spirit of the owner. By some business or professional community leader.)

AN AFFIRMATION OF FAITH: (Unison) (See page 130)

A LITANY OF DEDICATION

LEADER: To the recognition of God and the values of human brotherhood expressed in vital religion—

GROUP: We dedicate this funeral home.

LEADER: To the ministry of comfort and consolation in behalf of those who are bereaved—

GROUP: We dedicate this funeral home.

LEADER: To the efficient courteous and thoughtful handling of the last rites of our comrades in the flesh, from many creeds, from many walks of life—those who possess much of this world's goods or have small earthly possessions—

GROUP: We dedicate this funeral home.

LEADER: To provide a home, a sanctuary for family and friends of deceased comrades, where tributes of respect may be expressed in beauty, symmetry, silence, music, art in spoken word, kindly hand-clasp—

GROUP: We dedicate this funeral home.

LEADER: To offer love, comradeship, courage, patience, courtesy, mutual understanding and to provide noble fellowship—

GROUP: We dedicate this funeral home.

LEADER: To strengthen the ties of human brotherhood through an appropriate ministry in sorrow—

GROUP: We dedicate this Funeral Home and earnestly petition the Father of us all that the workmen from many skilled vocations who have wrought on this beautiful timely edifice may share with the owner and the community the deep satisfaction of this achievement.

DOXOLOGY

BENEDICTION

The Lord bless thee, and keep thee;

The Lord make his face to shine upon thee, and be gracious unto thee;

The Lord lift up his countenance upon thee, and give thee peace. Amen.—(Numbers 6:24-26)

RELIGIOUS OPENING AND DEDICATION
OF PLACE OF BUSINESS

PRELUDE OF ORGAN MUSIC

READING OF THE SCRIPTURES:

Unless the Lord builds the house, those who build it labor in vain. Unless the Lord watches over the city, the watchman stays awake in vain.—Psalm 127:1.

For no other foundation can anyone lay than that which is laid, which is Jesus Christ. Now if anyone builds on the foundation with gold, silver, precious stones, wood, hay, stubble—each man's work will become manifest; for the Day will disclose it because it will be revealed with fire, and the fire will test what sort of work each one has done. If the work which any man has built on the foundation survives, he will receive a reward.—I Corinthians 3:11-14.

INVOCATION:

Infinite God and Father of all, we thank Thee that Thou hast placed within the being of man a desire for aspiration and achievement. Thy creative work has challenged man, Thy creature whom Thou didst create a little lower than Thyself to build and expand and extend his services to his fellowmen that the blessings of convenience and comfort may be available to all, and that from this service human kind may derive a sense of dependence and brotherhood, community interest and concern, thus seeking to exemplify the spirit of Christ who is not only the Master builder of our faith, but of the framework of economic right and social blessedness. It is in His name that we invoke Thy blessing upon the religious opening and dedication of this place of business. Amen.

SPECIAL MUSIC: (Daughter of the owner of the business)

STATEMENT OF PURPOSE:

It is a most refreshing experience to pause in the midst of the onrushing demands of economic life in our community for the religious opening of this place of business. It is as though above the clamor and clangor of commerce and trade we have heard the voice of the Infinite calling to us—"Be still and know that I am God."

This religious opening is a living demonstration of the fact that economic ground can be holy ground. The fact that we draw near to God is an admission that worldly standards of good business are inadequate, and that Christianity is essential to the ethical and spiritual aspects of our economic life. By calling upon God at a moment such as this, we reject selfish materialism, and submit ourselves as God's stewards to meet the material issues of life squarely and reverently, for we know that the "earth is the Lord's and the fullness thereof, the world and they that dwell therein"; that God "hath made us, and we are His."

With these high purposes in mind let us pray:

PRAYER:

O Thou who art the eternal God, and Father of our Lord Jesus Christ, dwelling place of Thy people through the ages, art now and ever will be the pillar of our strength and the refuge of our spirits—conceive within us the sense of righteousness by which we may open this place of business. In the name of all that is just, honest, true, may those who own and manage, those who labor and serve, and those who buy and trade, be deeply aware of the creative satisfactions which enter the realm of business relations through the contributions which are made. May sincere appreciations be shown to those who are willing to invest capital in ventures which provide the very best in place

126

and goods, and, those who place their confidence and patronage in behalf of worthy investments and faith that human needs will thus be met.

O thou whose kingdom must first be sought, help us in the opening of this house of business to remember the words of our Lord, who said, "Know yet not that I must be about my Father's business?" May we understand that every Christian has a sacred calling in his occupation to serve God daily as an expression of his love and good will for his fellow men. As many people cross these thresholds, may the real purpose of their lives be to seek the Kingdom of God and His righteousness, that these things may be added unto them.

In the name of Christ, our Lord, we pray. Amen.

SUGGESTED LIST OF ANNIVERSARIES
TO BE OBSERVED*

(In addition to the regular anniversaries coming within the Christian Year, there are several other possibilities from which to choose. We might call them TIMELESS ANNIVERSARIES. It would be impossible to include them all.)

1. Golden Wedding Anniversary.

2. Hymn Festival. (Music Week—May).

3. Homecoming.

4. Law Observance and Enforcement Week.

5. Consecration of Newly-weds.

6. Flower Festival.

7. Retreat for Church Leadership.

8. Silver Wedding Anniversary.

9. Birthday Sunday. (First Sunday in June.)

10. Father and Son Banquet.

11. Mother and Daughter Banquet.

12. Harvest Festival.

13. Installation Day.

14. Historical Pageant.

15. Pioneer Day.

*Every local church, on close observation, will doubtless discover certain high days of interest, common only to that particular local church or community. These are in the midst of life. Point them up with appropriate emphasis.

A FORM FOR EASTER SUNRISE SERVICE

MEDLEY OF RESURRECTION HYMNS:

"Above the Hills of Time the Cross Is Gleaming"
"In the Cross of Christ I Glory"
"Christ the Lord Is Risen Today"
"Thine Is the Glory"
"I Know that My Redeemer Lives"

MEDITATION: (For a thoughtful moment of silence during the medley)

And very early on the first day of the week they went to the tomb when the sun had risen. And they were saying to one another, "Who will roll away the stone for us from the door of the tomb?" And looking up, they saw that the stone was rolled back for it was very large. And entering the tomb, they saw a young man sitting on the right side, dressed in a white robe; and they were amazed. And he said to them, "Do not be amazed; you seek Jesus of Nazareth, who was crucified. He has risen, he is not here; see the place where they laid him. *But go tell . . .* "

Mark 16:2-7.

THE SCRIPTURAL STORY OF THE RESURRECTION:

John 20:1-18 (Minister)

INVOCATION

THE POET SPEAKS OF THE RESURRECTION:

"What Does Easter Mean to You?". . .*Thomas Curtis Clark*

MEMORY GEMS FROM GOD'S WORD:

(Directed by Minister)

HYMN OF FAITH: "My Faith Looks Up to Thee"

SENTENCE PRAYERS: (Open to everyone)

A Brief Message: "As It Began to Dawn"
(Minister).

A New Testament Confession of Faith and
Statement of Loyalty: (Unison)

We believe that God is spirit and they that worship him
must worship in spirit and in truth.

We believe that God hath made of one blood all nations
of men to dwell on the face of the earth.

We believe that God is love and everyone that loveth
is born of God and knoweth God.

We believe that Jesus is the Son of God, and as many as
are led by the spirit of God, they are the sons of God.

We believe that the Lord Jesus is the Way, the Truth,
and the Life.

We believe that if we walk in the light as He is in the
light, we have fellowship one with another.

We believe that, if we confess our sins He is faithful and
just to forgive us our sins and to cleanse us from all
unrighteousness.

We believe that the world passeth away, and the lust
thereof; but that He that doeth the will of God abid-
eth forever.

—A Mosaic from the Gospel of John,
The Christian Evangelist.

Closing Hymn of Consecration:
"Take My Life and Let It Be"

Benediction:

FORM FOR A HOMECOMING SERVICE

(This service includes a mortgage-burning and personal dedication.)

PRELUDE:

"Andante Religioso".....*Arranged from Francis Thome*

CALL TO WORSHIP: (Standing) Chairman of the Board

According to the Scriptures it is right that man erect houses for the worship of God, and that they should be set apart and dedicated to religious uses. We are assembled here today for the purpose of dedicating this building to the worship and service of Almighty God. As we burn the mortgage we also rededicate ourselves to Christ.

LEADER: God is spirit, and those who worship Him must worship in spirit and truth.—John 4:24.

CONGREGATION: This is the day which the Lord has made; let us rejoice and be glad in it. I was glad when they said to me, "Let us go to the house of the Lord."

—Psalm 118:24; 122:1.

HYMN: "The Church's One Foundation," (1, 2).

PRAYER: (seated)

"THREE FOLD AMEN"

THE CHURCH: (By adult and youth leaders)

Foundation: Matthew 16:16-18

Organization: Acts 14:23

Teaching: Titus 2

Mission: Matthew 28:19-20

Preaching: Romans 10:14-15

DUET: "Praise Be Thine".................*Mendelssohn*

BURNING OF THE MORTGAGE:

(Chairman of the Board, or an Elder Emeritus, or President of the Christian Women's Fellowship)

LEADER: In the spirit of gratitude to our heavenly Father by whose favor, inspiration and guidance we have been able to free our church from all indebtedness;

CONGREGATION: We burn this mortgage.

LEADER: In love for our church home and in reverent memory of all those who by their services and sacrifices down through the years have bequeathed to us such a valuable church property;

CONGREGATION: We burn this mortgage.

LEADER: In grateful appreciation of the generosity of the members and friends of this church, the spirit of loyalty, unity and sacrifice manifested by the whole church in this achievement;

CONGREGATION: We burn this mortgage.

RESPONSE OF PRAISE:

> Holy, Holy, Holy, Lord God of Hosts!
> Heav'n and earth are full of Thee!
> Heav'n and earth are praising Thee,
> O Lord most High.
> (Refrain of "Day Is Dying in the West")

PERSONAL DEDICATION: (seated, heads bowed)

LEADER: In determination that we shall enlarge our vision and that through its minister, its elders, its deacons and its other faithful leaders this church shall serve more effectively in the days ahead;

CONGREGATION: We now dedicate ourselves, our services and our substance anew to the work of this our beloved church, and to the extension of the kingdom of Jesus Christ throughout this community, this nation and the wide world that the will of God may be done on earth as it is in heaven.

PRAYER OF DEDICATION: (standing) ...... (The Minister)

MUSIC: "Great Is Thy Faithfulness".............._Runyon_
(By Organist or mixed quartet)

SERMON: "The Church in the World Today"

BENEDICTION

CLOSING HYMN: "God Be With You Till We Meet Again"
(stanza only)

POSTLUDE

A MEMORIAL SERVICE FOR A STATE CONVENTION
Theme: "The Brotherhood Immortal"
(This service is suggested as a possible memorial portion within a State Convention Program. It should be short, full of meaning, deeply spiritual.)

ORGAN PRELUDE

PRAYER—IN MEMORIAM

"O Merciful Father, suffer none of us to live without hope; but constrain us mightily by Thy love: that we may be renewed by Thy grace, and be acceptable unto Thee through Christ. May we walk in newness of life. We pray that those who were numbered among us, who served Thee in their generation, may be gathered unto Thee in the confidence of their faith. Make the night of this world's grief be lighted by Thy presence. In the name of Christ we pray." Amen.

HYMN: "My Faith Looks Up to Thee"

RESPONSIVE SCRIPTURE READING: (John 14:1-16)
(This may be used as a unison reading if preferred—print it in your bulletin.)

A MOMENT OF SILENCE:
(A thought from General Lew Wallace may guide our meditation—"The monuments of the nations are all protests against nothingness after death; so are statues and inscriptions; so is history.")

PRAYER: (in unison)
Our Father, we thank Thee for the Church, in which we find one of life's greatest fellowships. We thank Thee for those who caught the Spirit of Christ, and have walked with Thee. We thank Thee for their faithfulness to duty, their devotion, their courage, and that we were privileged to share with them in the life of the Church. In their memory we gather at this moment to voice our tribute of

memory and appreciation. For these comrades of the faith we thank Thee. In the name of Christ. Amen.

TO THESE AND MANY OTHERS WE OFFER
TRIBUTE IN MEMORY:

(List names of ministers)

. . . .

. . . .

. . . .

(A list is always fragmentary and inadequate. Your memory will supply names of women, men, officers, mothers, fathers)

QUIET MUSIC:

"Sunset and Evening Star". . . . .*Tennyson and Barnby*
(No. 574 in *Christian Worship*)

BRIEF DEVOTIONAL ADDRESS: "The Brotherhood Immortal" (Preferably by some outstanding minister—elderly—in whom all have great confidence.)

BENEDICTION:

Now may the God of peace, who brought again from the dead our Lord Jesus, the great shepherd of the sheep, by the blood of the eternal covenant, equip you with everything good that you may do his will, working in you that which is pleasing in his sight, through Jesus Christ; to whom be glory forever and ever. Amen.

(Hebrews 13:20, 21)

CHAPTER IV

THE MINISTER GUIDES CHURCH PROCEDURES

Christian Baptism.

The Lord's Supper.

Communion Meditations.

Communion Prayers.

A Special Service of the Lord's Supper.

Transfer of Membership.

A Church Covenant.

A Commissioning Service.   (1)   (2)

A Mortgage Burning

A Farewell Service in an Old Church Building.

Articles of Incorporation.

Additional Suggestions.

ADMINISTERING CHRISTIAN BAPTISM

1. SUGGESTIONS

The Christian Ordinance of Baptism can be so administered as to be a beautiful and impressive symbol. In addition to being an act of obedience it is a dramatic act which vividly pictures the death, burial and resurrection of Christ. Careless and indifferent administration is inexcusable.

Every congregation should have a baptistry inside the sanctuary, located in the chancel so that the focal point of attention on entering the church will be the two Christian ordinances, the Lord's Supper and Christian Baptism, and provision for their meaningful observance. The baptistry should be beautiful and of adequate dimensions. There should be an abundant supply of leaded robes for both sexes. This lends dignity and impressiveness. The water in the baptistry should be heated. The ordinance should be approached with hymns and prayer.

The following service, if followed with care and dignity, will insure a beautiful administration of the ordinance. If you need instruction about the details of baptizing, ask an older minister.

Do not hurry. Always finish the reading of Scripture, or the singing of a verse of song before baptizing the candidate. Select a good reader. Let the congregation sing appropriate hymns while the minister and candidates are making the necessary preparation. Have a robe or cloak to throw over the shoulders of a woman candidate as she comes from the water. With these suggestions well in mind, familiarize yourself with the following service.

2. A BAPTISMAL SERVICE

(Someone appointed to read:)

And Jesus came and said to them, "All authority in heaven and on earth has been given to me. Go therefore and make disciples of all nations, baptizing them in the name of the Father and of the Son and of the Holy Spirit, teaching them to observe all that I have commanded you; and lo, I am with you always, to the close of the age."—Matthew 28:18-20.

Prayer.

(The minister leads the first candidate into the water and some-one, preferably an elder, reads.)

And they both went down into the water, Philip and the Eunuch, and he baptized him.—Acts 8:38.

(The candidate is then baptized, and the reader or minister says:)

Jesus answered him, "Truly, truly, I say to you, unless one is born anew, he cannot see the kingdom of God." Nicodemus said to him, "How can a man be born when he is old? Can he enter a second time into his mother's womb and be born?" Jesus answered, "Truly, truly, I say to you, unless one is born of water and the Spirit, he cannot enter the kingdom of God."—John 3:3-5.

(As the second candidate is led into the water, the minister, or reader, shall say:)

And Peter said to them, "Repent, and be baptized every one of you in the name of Jesus Christ for the forgiveness of your sins; and you shall receive the gift of the Holy Spirit."

—Acts 2:38.

(As the candidate is lowered into the water, a familiar hymn is sung, or the choir uses one of the baptismal chants.)

(After the third baptism, the minister says:)

And you were buried with Him in baptism, in which you were also raised with Him through faith in the working of God, who raised Him from the dead . . . If then you have been raised with Christ, seek the things that are above, where Christ is, seated at the right hand of God. Set your mind on things that are above, not on things that are on earth. For you have died and your life is hid with Christ in God.

—Colossians 2:12; 3:1-3.

(As the fourth candidate is lowered into the water, another verse is sung, or the choir chants.)

(As the fifth candidate enters the baptistry, the minister, or reader, says:)

In those days came John the Baptist, preaching in the wilderness of Judea, "Repent, for the kingdom of heaven is at hand . . ." Then went out to him Jerusalem and all Judea and all the region about the Jordan, and they were baptized by him in the River Jordan, confessing their sins.—Matthew 3:1, 2, 5, 6.

(The fifth candidate is then baptized, and the choir sings, or the reader says:)

Then came Jesus from Galilee to the Jordan to John, to be baptized by him. John would have prevented him saying, "I need to be baptized by you, and do you come to me?" But Jesus answered him, "Let it be so now; for thus it is fitting for us to fulfill all righteousness." Then he consented. And when Jesus was baptized he went up immediately from the water, and behold the heavens were opened and he saw the Spirit of God descending like a dove and alighting on him; and lo a voice from heaven, saying, "This is my beloved Son, with whom I am well pleased."—Matthew 3:13-17.

(The sixth candidate is baptized, after which a stanza or two of a hymn is sung.)

(As the seventh candidate rises from the water, the minister, or preferably the reader, says:)

What shall we say then? Are we to continue in sin that grace may abound? By no means! How can we who died to sin still live in it? Do you not know that all of us who have been baptized into Christ Jesus were baptized into His death? We were buried therefore with him by baptism into death, so that as Christ was raised from the dead by the glory of the Father, we too might walk in newness of life.—Romans 6:1-4.

(The eighth candidate is then baptized, and as he rises from the water a hymn is sung until the ninth candidate is in the baptistry.)

(As the ninth candidate is baptized, the reader says:)

For if we have been united with Him in a death like His, we shall certainly be united with Him in a resurrection like His. We know that our old self was crucified with Him so that the sinful body might be destroyed, and we might no longer be enslaved to sin. For he who has died is freed from sin. But if we have died with Christ, we believe that we shall also live with Him. For we know that Christ being raised from the dead will never die again; death no longer has dominion over him. The death He died He died to sin, once for all, but the life He lives He lives to God. So you also must consider yourselves dead to sin and alive to God in Christ Jesus.

(If there are other candidates, use hymns or chants during the intermissions between baptisms.)

(After the last candidate is baptized, the minister says:)

And being made perfect he became the source of eternal salvation to all who obey him.—Hebrews 5:9.

For in Christ Jesus you are all sons of God, through faith. For as many of you as were baptized into Christ have put on Christ.—Galatians 3:26-27.

(In closing, let all sing "O Master, Let Me Walk With Thee"— [Tune, Maryton]. Then follows the benediction.)

(If desired, a folder may be prepared giving the above Scripture readings on baptism, and the congregation may read in unison as the service proceeds.)

3. BAPTISMAL FORMULAS

By the authority of the Glorified Head of the church, I baptize you (using the given name of the candidate, or the words, "my brother", "my sister," "my child,") in the name of the Father, and of the Son, and of the Holy Spirit. Amen.

or

In obedience to the Great Commission and upon profession of your faith in the Lord Jesus Christ, I baptize you (same as above) in the name of the Father, and of the Son, and of the Holy Spirit. Amen.

or

Upon confession of your faith in Jesus as the Christ, the Son of God, and your Saviour, I baptize you in the name of the Father, and of the Son, and of the Holy Spirit. Amen.

or

Upon your profession of "repentance toward God and of faith in the Lord Jesus Christ," I baptize you in the name of the Father, and of the Son, and of the Holy Spirit. Amen.

PRAYER BEFORE BAPTISM

We give Thee thanks, O God, for those who have accepted our Lord Jesus Christ as Saviour and who now are to put on Christ, in His own appointed way. Receive them, O Lord, according to the promise offered through Thy well beloved Son. May they go with Him into this likeness of His death and rise to walk with Him in the new life. Grant that these and all of us may enjoy the benediction of the everlasting life with Thee, in the promised home above. In Christ, we pray. Amen.

PRAYER AFTER BAPTISM

Holy and righteous Father, whose beloved Son, Christ Jesus, for the forgiveness of sin, did shed His precious blood and gave commandment to His disciples; that they should teach all nations, and baptize them in the name of the Father and of the Son and of the Holy Spirit; hear our prayer for these who have been baptized. May they be faithful to the covenant of Christians, may they receive the fullness of Thy grace, and finally the gift of eternal life in and through Jesus Christ, our Lord. Amen.

Now to Him who is able to keep you from falling and to present you without blemish before the presence of His glory with rejoicing, to the only God, our Saviour through Jesus Christ our Lord, be glory, majesty, dominion and authority before all time, and now, for ever. Amen. — Jude 1:24, 25.

OBSERVING THE LORD'S SUPPER
"HIS DAY—HIS HOUSE—HIS TABLE—HIS PEOPLE"

It is the Lord's Table, which the church as His bride prepares for Him. In the observance of the Lord's Supper we have the perfect blending of physical things and the vision of God. The bread and the wine are physical. At the institution of the Lord's Supper in the Upper Room in Jerusalem, they were simply the leftovers from the meal. But whenever and wherever men of spiritual discernment gather at the Table of His Presence and observe this Christian ordinance, something more than bread, something more than wine is there.

It is the custom of the Christian Church, following Apostolic example, to observe the Lord's Supper on the first day of the week. "Let a man examine himself, and so eat of the bread and drink of the cup."—I Corinthians 11:28. This is the attitude in which we should approach this memorial feast.

The minister should use his good offices to see that the Table is properly dressed, with clean linen, clean vessels for the emblems and upright men for the service. It is wise for the minister to work out with the officers of the church a dignified routine that the observance may be free from awkward mistakes. The size of the congregation to be served is a determining factor. Normal procedure would call for three elders at the table, one of them (or the minister) may preside, the other two give the prayers.

FORM OF OBSERVANCE

After two stanzas of a communion hymn have been sung, the Lord's Table shall be uncovered. Then the one who is presiding will read a portion of Scripture, give a brief statement in prose or in poetry setting forth the importance of this memorial, and say:

For I received from the Lord what I also delivered to you, that the Lord Jesus on the night when he was betrayed took bread, and when He had given thanks, He broke it, and said, "This is my body which is for you. Do this in remembrance of me." In the same way also the cup, after supper, saying, "This cup is the new covenant in my blood. Do this, as often as you drink it, in remembrance of me." For as often as you eat this bread and drink the cup you proclaim the Lord's death until He comes.—I Corinthians 11:23-26.

The elders then give the plates of bread into the hands of the deacons, also trays containing the cups. The elders are served by the deacons nearest them, the others proceed to their assigned section of the congregation and serve the people. After all have been served the deacons will come to the front again with plates and trays, they will be served by the elders, and all officers will be seated in their accustomed places. A third stanza of the communion hymn, sung at this time, will seal this portion of the worship service to its intended place and purpose.

In many churches the morning offering is received immediately following the Communion Service. It is preferable to have the offering before rather than after the Lord's Supper.

Millions of Christian people in churches of many religious bodies unite in the observance of the Lord's Supper on World-Wide Communion Sunday, the first Sunday in October. The manner in which the observance is carried through may differ widely. Some may have the prayer for the loaf, then pass it, then the prayer for the cup and pass it—others may have all partake simultaneously of the loaf, then in like manner the cup—others may have the people come forward to the Table (Altar) for partaking. In any event, the purpose is the same and we rejoice in the growing spirit of unity and understanding.

COMMUNION MEDITATIONS FROM THE NEW TESTAMENT

Matthew 26:26-28
Mark 14:22-26
Luke 22:19-22
I Corinthians 11:23-26
John 14 (Selections)
Romans 8:35-39
Romans 12:1-3
I Corinthians 13 (Selections)
Ephesians 4:1-6
Ephesians 6:10-18 (Selections)
Philippians 2:5-11
Philippians 3:7-10
Philippians 4:8,9
Colossians 3:15-17

FOR THE LOAF

1. Our Father, we come to the Table of Thy Presence in the spirit of sincere humility. As we examine our hearts we feel unworthy of the supreme sacrifice made for our salvation.

Give us today, as we partake of the loaf, a deeper understanding and a new resolve. May this symbol of the broken body of Thy Son have enriched meaning, and may it give us courage toward greater sacrifices on our part, that Thy Kingdom may come on earth among men. In His name we pray. Amen.

2. Gracious Father, we gather today at this, the longest Table in the world, that side by side with comrades of all races and nations, we may feel deeply Thy Holy Presence. Open our eyes, we pray, to the noblest visions, the highest aspirations, the deepest convictions of the Christian life as we partake of this loaf. May this manna from on high give us spiritual strength that Thy spirit may control us in thought, word and deed. This we pray in the Master's name. Amen.

3. Our Father, in the fullness of joy on the glorious resurrection day, we pause for a few moments of thoughtful communion around Thy Table spread with the symbols of sacrifice.

Help us to understand that earth's saddest day, and earth's gladdest day were only one day apart. May we find in both days Thy prevailing love. Let this loaf appropriately remind us of the broken body of our suffering Lord. May these moments of communion quicken within us the spirit of humility, and give us a sincere desire to show more love toward Thee by unselfish service.

This we pray in the name of our Risen Redeemer, even Jesus the Christ. Amen.

1.   Continuing our thanksgiving, our Father, we would voice our great satisfaction in this quiet moment of communion. In the delightful beauty of this worshipful sanctuary we assemble about this memorial Table. May we find in this cup, so expressive, so reassuring of Thy love and sacrifice, a challenge to steadfastness in daily Christian living, Grant to each worshipper here today enrichment of spirit, as we share this memorial experience. In Christ's holy name, we pray. Amen.

2.   Our Father, may we find in these moments of intimate fellowship around Thy Table spiritual strength to overcome our many weaknesses. May we be sincere and true. Help us as we take of the fruit of the vine, symbolizing the life blood of Thy Son, to grow more worthy, to become more thoughtful, to be more willing to share thy never-ending love with others. Give us open minds, receptive hearts, conquering spirits, that we may become more and more like the sinless Master, in whose name we pray. Amen.

3.   Our Father, we read in Thy Word that without the shedding of blood there can be no remission of sins. As we take of the cup of suffering today may we be reminded of Calvary and the supreme sacrifice made by our Master upon the cross. Give us understanding hearts and minds. Quicken within us the desire to prove our sincerity as those who wear the name of Christ and who desire to serve him consistently.

We would therefore together in this high moment of worship renew our vows of loyalty to Thy Kingdom. Forgive us in our weaknesses. Strengthen us in our noble purposes. This we pray in the name of Christ our sinless Master. Amen.

A SERVICE OF THE LORD'S SUPPER

ORGAN PRELUDE AND PROCESSIONAL:
"Adagio" .... *Mendelssohn*

CALL TO WORSHIP AND INVOCATION

HYMN OF WORSHIP: "Praise to the Lord, the Almighty"

LITANY OF CHALLENGE

LEADER

Holy Father, in the name of him who said, "For their sakes I consecrate myself"; we come to consecrate ourselves to thee for the sake of all men.

RESPONSE

We dedicate ourselves, O God.

Thou light of all minds, who hast endowed us with intellects, and hast designed us to think thy thoughts after thee:

We dedicate our minds to thee, O God.

Thou lover of the souls of all, whose sympathy, compassion and affection were bestowed without stint and willest that our hearts burn with zeal in the service of our brothers:

We dedicate and discipline our emotions for thy sake and theirs, O God.

Spirit of truth, who hast endowed us with the power of moral choice, and callest us to climb the heights of thy way for our lives;

We dedicate our wills to thee, O God.

To the Christian enterprise throughout the earth, and to the acceptance of our full stewardship;

We dedicate ourselves.

To securing economic rights for all; to the gaining of justice for exploited minorities; and to the acceptance of our responsibilities as world citizens,

We dedicate ourselves.

To the relief of all suffering peoples; to ministering to the impoverished; to the application of the ethics of Christ in building a Christian world order;

We dedicate ourselves.

To the establishment of Christ's way in our business, family, and individual relationships as a token of his desired order for all men;

We dedicate ourselves.

UNISON

Holy and eternal God, maker of heaven and earth, and Father of our souls, who hast called us to be fellow workers with thee, and hast given us each a work to do; take our lives and let them be consecrated, Lord, to thee, for the sake of, and in the spirit of him who came not to be ministered to, but to minister, and to give his life for many, even Jesus Christ our Lord.

GLORIA PATRI

COMMUNION HYMN: "Here at Thy Table Lord" (vs. 1, 2)

COMMUNION MEDITATION

SPECIAL MUSIC: "Let Us Break Bread Together"

WORDS OF INSTITUTION AND PRAYERS

DISTRIBUTION OF THE ELEMENTS

HYMN OF THANKSGIVING: "Now Thank We All Our God"

BENEDICTION

POSTLUDE: "Sonata" . . . . Mendelssohn

TRANSFER OF MEMBERSHIP
CHURCH LETTERS

Church letters are not so much in common usage as they were a number of years ago. This is due in part to delays in the process of issuing letters, and the further fact that they reveal so little about the individual member and his qualities of character. We usually depend on a "statement of standing" given orally by the one who comes forward to take membership, having been a member elsewhere. Again, some church letters have found lodgement in a trunk rather than in the church near the new place of residence. If a letter is sent, it should follow a reasonable form, such as the one offered herewith, and if an additional word of commendation can be given let it be of a more personal nature. A church letter should be authorized by the board of one church and sent to the minister of another church, not from church to an individual. When the individual takes membership in another church that church should, through common courtesy, notify the church from which the member comes.

FORM OF CHURCH LETTER

THE CHRISTIAN CHURCH (Disciples) at.................

To the Disciples of Christ, wherever this may be presented: Greeting:

THIS IS TO CERTIFY

That the bearer.........................is a member with us in good standing and full fellowship and as such we cordially commend............to your Christian love and guidance.

By Order of the Church, this........day of...........
19.....

...................................Church Clerk

(To such letters this word could be added.)

The bearer will be considered a member of this congregation until we are notified of the reception elsewhere.

148

(To such letters this alternate word might be added.)

If notified within six months of this reception by you he will be considered as transferred, otherwise this letter is null and void.

(This coupon could very acceptably be attached for the convenience of the Clerk of the Church granting the letter:)

To..............................

This is to certify that.........................has

united with the Church at......................on the

........day of.........................19.....

.....................................Clerk

ADJUSTMENT OF DIFFICULTIES AND PROBLEMS

It must needs be that offenses come and the wise minister is put to no greater test of his tact, his wisdom, and his moral courage than in dealing with them.

Remember, that the way of doing a thing is quite as important as the thing itself. Be wise as serpents and harmless as doves.

Do nothing, say nothing, write nothing that you would not be perfectly willing to have known. Trust very few people with confidences that you would not have made public, for in the day and the hour when you think not they will be made public.

The instructions of the Master in regard to offenses (Matthew 18:15-17) are intensely practical and practicable.

If the offense is public in character, let the elders follow the course there laid down.

If a man thinks he is not justly dealt with, let a committee mutually agreed upon hear and judge the matter.

If a church is disturbed and too many are involved for it to settle the matter of itself, let a sister church be invited to send a committee to advise.

Let all difficulties be approached in the spirit of brotherly love, Christian courtesy and kindness; in an effort to win and not to drive away, and, most difficulties can be settled—especially if prayer is constantly employed toward guidance and control. Your State Secretary will give all possible guidance, but the final decisions must be made locally.

CERTIFICATE OR CREDENTIAL FOR CONVENTION

There is a growing sentiment in favor of a delegate convention, that our conventions may be more representative in character. The following form may be used. Have it filled out by the clerk or minister of the church and taken to the Convention and deposited with the committee on credentials.

FORM OF CERTIFICATE

This is to certify that the bearer......................
is a duly chosen and properly authorized representative of

the......................church of..................
to the State Convention of Christian Churches to convene in

.... from .... 19......

The approximate membership of this church is...........

and........representatives have been chosen.

Signed................................

Date........................

A CHURCH COVENANT

(It is suggested that when a new congregation is
being organized, a Covenant may be entered into
that the congregation may be identified and the
general direction of activities agreed upon. In
many instances a new congregation—or one pre-
viously established—may desire to adopt a Constitution and By-Laws. This action would go beyond
the confines of a Covenant and would deal with
administration and program of the church.)

COVENANT

According to the New Testament, Jesus who is called the
Christ, laid the foundation for the beginning of His Church
through His birth, life, ministry, death, burial and resurrection. This plan culminated on the Day of Pentecost.

Within the pattern of the New Testament Church we
discover two Christian Ordinances—(1) Baptism the initial
rite, by which through obedience the penitent believer drama-
tizes his new relationship to Christ as he enacts the death,
burial and resurrection of the Lord Jesus Christ. (2) The
Lord's Supper, instituted on the night before His betrayal, by
which Christians "as often as they partake" are reminded of
the suffering and sacrificial death of Christ upon the cross,
that the world might be redeemed.

We, the members of . . . . Church
of . . . . , a congregationally-governed
body, in order to promote the work of the church in the
spirit of Christ, and thus advance His Kingdom, do this day
covenant and agree that together we will strive to bring in His
Kingdom on earth. We acknowledge affiliation with the
Brotherhood known as the Christian Church (Disciples of

Christ), and committed to the historic principles of this body whose local churches are variously known as Christian Churches, Churches of Christ, or Disciples of Christ.

It is further understood that this congregation is actively affiliated with the United Christian Missionary Society, the State Board of Christian Churches, Unified Promotion, and other agencies well known in brotherhood life.

The purpose of this local church shall be, as revealed in the New Testament, to win people to faith in Jesus Christ and commit them actively to growth in grace and in knowledge of Christ, that increasingly they may know and do His will. To work for the unity of all Christians, and, with them engage in the building of the Kingdom of God.

The membership of this congregation shall consist of those who are now identified as members of this church, and, those who shall unite with it by primary obedience, or by transfer of membership. For this purpose and to this end we hereby attach our signatures to this

COVENANT

. . . .

. . . .

. . . .

(As many lines may be added as needed)
(Adaptations of the above are often appropriate)

SING THE UNIVERSAL SONG

(Tune: "Jesus Saves")

Sing the universal song,

    Unity, unity;

Churches unified are strong,

    Unity, unity;

Jesus prayed that we be one,

That men might believe the Son,

And his glorious work be done,

    Unity, unity.

Sing one God, one church, one plan,

    Unity, unity;

And one cross for every man,

    Unity, unity;

Build love's ramparts where hate stood,

Share the joy and truth and good

In one world of brotherhood,

    Unity, unity. Amen.

—Chauncey R. Piety

FORM FOR A COMMISSIONING SERVICE

When the spirit of Evangelism arises in a well-established congregation and the need for a group of qualified leaders to form the nucleus of a new church is imminent, it is time to consider a Commissioning Service. This strategy is often employed in a city when new residential sections are in the building process. The group to be commissioned should be volunteers who are devoted Christians with poise and experience.

When the names of the group to be commissioned are in hand, they should be called together by the minister and elders of the church and the plan explained, the need made clear, the purpose outlined. If the individuals and families in the volunteer group, who in most instances live in the area of the new congregation, agree to the Commissioning Service, plans may then be consummated and a period of time, preferably in the morning hour of worship, designated as the time. Full announcement should be made ahead of time. A brief service may follow this pattern—

READING OF THE GREAT COMMISSION:

Matthew 28:18-20; Acts 1:1-8.

HYMN: "I Love Thy Kingdom, Lord" (Standing)

ROLL CALL OF THOSE TO BE COMMISSIONED:

(As each name is called, the person will stand and remain standing until all names have been called, then all may be seated.)

STATEMENT BY MINISTER OR ELDER:

(This word will indicate the need for the new congregation, the willingness of the group to leave the home church to help form the new, the agreement of the home church to send them forth, the challenge of growth, willingness to serve, opportunity to witness, possibility of success in the new enterprise.)

VOTE OF CONFIDENCE AND APPROVAL BY THE
CONGREGATION:

(The entire congregation, other than those to be commissioned, will stand at the request of the minister, then be seated.)

CHARGE TO EVERYONE: (Minister or elder)

To you, who are today being commissioned for a very important service in the Kingdom of God, we offer our sincere blessing and send you forth as ambassadors from the mother church to assist in the establishment of a new church. You will carry with you the good will, the prayers, and blessing of this congregation from which you embark on this mission of Christian service. You will represent initiative, experience, spiritual and financial resources, so greatly needed in the new church........................(name) in which you will serve. As Paul and his companions went out from the Antioch church with the blessing of the home church upon them, even so you are going forth today with a vision and a personal consecration to this given task.

To the members of this congregation which remain, and have expressed your willingness for these to be commissioned, may I request that you spend much time in prayer in behalf of this group. Possibly some of you who also live in the area of the new church may want to join these in their sacrificial efforts. If so, although we will greatly miss you as we miss them, but our loss is someone else's gain. As Christians we face the call of the Master. Each one must answer for himself. You will be called upon to aid financially in the establishment of the new church. Your worthy record in the past speaks for your willingness to give needed support now. All of us today rejoice in Christian forward movements. Blessings upon you all.

HYMN OF CONSECRATION: "O Jesus I Have Promised"

CLOSING PRAYER OF COMMITMENT: (Elder)

> NOTE: If wisdom dictates, the entire congregation may then have a fellowship meal together, in the fellowship hall of the commissioning church, or on the plot of ground where the new church is to be built.

One church issued a 2½ x 4 inch card to each family, reading like this—

The....................Christian Church

(City) ....

COMMISSIONS

....

to go forth and establish a new Christian Congregation in.....................to be known as

The .... Christian Church

....

(Chairman of the Board)   (Minister)

Here is a larger form for the Commissioning Service—

SERVICE OF COMMISSIONING

(Date) ....

The....................Christian Church

(Place) ....

hereby

COMMISSIONS

....

To go forth and establish a new Christian Congregation in.....................to be known as

The .... Christian Church

"Go Ye therefore, and make disciples . . . "

Matthew 28:19

....

(Chairman of the Board)   (Minister)

(The picture of the commissioning church is shown in a light ink drawing in the center of this certificate. This is issued to the group as a whole.)

ANOTHER COMMISSIONING SERVICE
MORNING WORSHIP

HYMN OF PRAISE: (selected)

LORD'S PRAYER

CHORAL RESPONSE

SERVICE OF COMMISSIONING

Call to Commissioning: (Minister First Church)

Hymn: "The Church's One Foundation"
(During the singing of this hymn twenty-nine members of First Church, and the minister and family of the new church came down the central isle and were seated at the front.)

Presentation of Certificates of Commissioning:
(By chairman of the First Church Board)

Prayer of Commissioning: (Oldest living member of First Church)

Hymn: "Lead On O King Eternal"—(During this hymn the minister and family of the new church followed by the twenty-nine members of First Church marched down the aisle and on to the temporary location of the new church.)

Message: (Minister of new church)

Invitation: (The twenty-nine placed membership in the new church and two others made the good confession.)

BENEDICTION

FORM FOR A SERVICE OF MORTGAGE BURNING

(This service may be enriched or shortened to fit the available time schedule and the local need.)

PRELUDE

OPENING SENTENCES: (Minister)

> I was glad when they said to me,
> "Let us go to the house of the Lord "
> Our feet have been standing
> within your gates, O Jerusalem
> Jerusalem, built as a city
> which is bound firmly together,
> to which the tribes go up, the
> tribes of the Lord . . .
> to give thanks to the name of the Lord.
> —Psalm 122:1-4

"Today is not yesterday. We ourselves change; how can our works and thoughts, if they are always to be the fittest, continue always the same? Change, indeed is painful, yet ever needful; and if memory have its force and worth, so also has hope." —Thomas Carlyle

HYMN OF PRAISE: "Come Thou Almighty King"

INVOCATION: (Minister)

BRIEF HISTORY OF THE CONGREGATION AND
    ITS BUILDING: (Chairman of the Board)
(Include here the date of organization, first building, present building, personnel.)

SCRIPTURE READING: (Matthew 21:12,13; Luke
        4:16-22a—President of the Christian
        Women's Fellowship)

HYMN: "I Love Thy Kingdom, Lord"

KINDLING THE FIRE

(A brief statement by the minister, pointing out the use of fire in a symbolic sense. Some fires are destructive, and others are constructive, etc., etc.)

(The Church treasurer will then burn the mortgage on a tray provided, on a table near the pulpit, or at least within sight of all assembled.) *

DOXOLOGY: (standing)

CLOSING PRAYER: (Chairman of the Building
Committee)

*Legally, it would be a safeguard to burn a substitute paper rather than the actual mortgage. The symbolism is the idea. The event is the high point of inspiration.

FOR THE FAREWELL SERVICE IN AN OLD CHURCH BUILDING

NOTE: It is suggested that the regular morning worship be conducted as usual, then follow with this service of farewell in the old sanctuary.

THE MINISTER PRESIDING

A STATEMENT FROM THE CHAIR-
MAN OF THE BOARD

A WORD FROM THE CHAIRMAN OF
THE BUILDING COMMITTEE

A LITANY OF GRATITUDE AND REJOICING

MINISTER: For the many years of service this church house has given and for the hallowed associations it brings to mind in the hearts of those who have worshiped here through the years.

CONGREGATION: We give Thee, our Father, a sincere word of gratitude.

MINISTER: For the children, youth and adults whose lives have been enriched by the varied activities of this congregation centered in this church house.

CONGREGATION: We would offer unto Thee our sincere gratitude for Christian growth.

MINISTER: For the devoted lives of ministers, musicians, evangelists, and other servants of the church who have invested their leadership abilities here.

CONGREGATION: We give Thee our heartfelt thanks.

MINISTER: For generous souls within the church and community who made possible the erection of this building and the maintenance of its activities through the years.

CONGREGATION: We are indeed grateful.

MINISTER: For the achievement of a new church home, representing progress, generous giving, deep consecration in which we will continue the Kingdom program of this congregation.

CONGREGATION: We would rejoice with hearts attune to gladness and with songs of praise on our lips.

UNISON: Today, our Father, our hearts and voices unite in gratitude and rejoicing for the Christian privileges we share on this notable day, and we would pledge to Thee a deeper, broader, higher, lengthier spirit of service in the name of Christ, whose we are and whom we serve. Amen.

BENEDICTION

ARTICLES OF INCORPORATION

Increasingly, our churches are finding that incorporation is wise procedure. At least three reasons may be offered to warrant incorporation:

1. Suppose that someone should be injured within the church house, or on church property, or in the event a loan should be outstanding against the church, and its doors were to be closed, the trustees would be held personally responsible unless the church is incorporated.

2. To make sure the church property is not lost to individuals, or agencies, not affiliated with the Brotherhood.

3. To make it possible to receive funds through bequests, or wills.

The matter of incorporation should be placed in the hands of a competent, Christian attorney, to draw up the legal document known as the Articles of Incorporation.

ADDITIONAL SUGGESTIONS

In guiding church procedures, the minister will find himself face to face with problems of administration, building a Church staff, establishing a cabinet, operating the church on a currently accepted organizational basis, setting up the official board for effective operation, providing a Constitution and By-Laws for orderly procedure, or developing a program of leadership training to meet the need in the local church.

It is not possible to cover these fields adequately in this *Service Manual*. The changing scenes in local church circles and the wider fields of Christian cooperation call for constant reading of church literature found in books, magazines, booklets dealing specifically with the problem or procedure of immediate concern.

The compiler of these chapters "bows out" at this point recognizing the limitations of this volume, in relation to appropriate procedures, and recommends that you correspond with your Brotherhood headquarters for current literature geared to your needs.

CHAPTER V

THE MINISTER AS A LEADER OF PUBLIC WORSHIP

BUILDING APPROPRIATE ORDERS
OF WORSHIP

(There is no place where one can show good taste
more definitely than in building and conducting
the public worship services of the church. In
some churches where a logical, psychological, sat-
isfactory order of worship is now in use, this
current practice has been achieved through a long
period of experimentation—evolution, if you want
to call it that. An adequate order of worship does
not just happen, neither is it a matter of hurriedly
throwing items together. The two orders of worship which follow, one for a church with a membership of approximately two thousand or more,
the other for a church with less than one hundred
members, are offered as suggestions. They have
been developed through the years. Build your
own slowly, securely, appropriately in the light
of your local situation, personnel, equipment.)

AN ORDER OF SERVICE FOR A CHURCH OF
TWO THOUSAND

ORGAN PRELUDE

(Your silence during this period will assist those who desire
to begin this hour of worship with music and reverent meditation.)

INTROIT

(A responsive introit, with sentences of Scripture given from
the Lectern, and a response by a hidden choir.)

PROCESSIONAL HYMN: (All standing)

ORGAN INTERLUDE

CALL TO WORSHIP: (responsive, print words)
(Congregation seated)

CHORALE (Choir and Congregation) (seated)

> ("O Thou by Whom We Come to God," etc.,
> or another of your choice)

THE LORD'S PRAYER

THREEFOLD AMEN . . . .*Choir*

ORGAN INTERLUDE

READING OF THE SCRIPTURE: (from Lectern)

CALL TO PRAISE

> Leader: O Lord, open Thou our lips.
>
> Choir: and our mouths shall show forth thy praise.
>
> Leader: Praise ye the Lord.
>
> Choir: The Lord's Name be praised. Amen.

GLORIA PATRI: (standing)

ANTHEM

ORGAN INTERLUDE

CALL TO PRAYER

> Minister: The Lord be with you.
>
> People: And with thy spirit.
>
> Minister: Let us pray.

HYMN: "Bless the Lord" . . . .*Choir*

PASTORAL PRAYER

SEVENFOLD AMEN . . . .*Choir*

Offering Service

    Offertory Sentence

    Offertory or Offertory Anthem

    Doxology (standing)

    Dedication and Choral Response

Communion Hymn: (stanzas 1 and 2)

The Lord's Supper

    (This is a feast of remembrance and fellowship. Any who wish are invited to partake of the loaf and cup, which are symbolic of the life and suffering of our Master and which suggest a spiritual union with all His followers.)

Hymn: (standing)

Sermon

Hymn of Invitation and Consecration

Benediction

"The Gift of Peace:" (The Lord bless thee, etc.)
Choir

Postlude

    NOTE: This service moves forward without hesitation and requires only one hour and ten minutes—often is completed within an hour. The introit, responses, etc., serve as enrichment. Congregational participation is ample.

AN ORDER OF SERVICE FOR A SMALL CHURCH

PRELUDE: (familiar hymns)

CALL TO WORSHIP: (Usually responsive, often given
by the minister)

HYMN OF PRAISE: (standing)

INVOCATION AND THE LORD'S PRAYER

SCRIPTURE READING: (seated)

THE MORNING PRAYER

OFFERING

    Sentence of Scripture

    Offering received

    Doxology

    Prayer of Dedication

COMMUNION

    Hymn: (stanzas 1 and 2)

    The Lord's Supper

    Hymn: (same as above, another stanza)

HYMN

MORNING MESSAGE

HYMN OF INVITATION AND CONSECRATION

BENEDICTION

SENTENCES FOR OPENING SERVICE OF WORSHIP
(To be quoted by the minister)

1

Blessed is he whom thou dost choose and
bring near,
to dwell in thy courts!
We shall be satisfied with the goodness
of thy house,
thy holy temple!   —Psalm 65:4

166

2

Come to me, all who labor and are heavy laden, and I will give you rest. Take my yoke upon you, and learn from me; for I am gentle and lowly in heart, and you will find rest for your souls. For my yoke is easy and my burden is light.

—Matthew 11:28-30

3

Hear, O Israel: The Lord our God is one Lord; and you shall love the Lord your God with all your heart, and with all your soul, and with all your might.　　—Deuteronomy 6:4,5

4

It is good to give thanks to the Lord,
　　to sing praises to thy name, O Most High;
to declare thy steadfast love in the morning,
　　and thy faithfulness by night.

—Psalm 92:1,2

5

O come, let us sing to the Lord;
　　let us make a joyful noise to the
　　rock of our salvation!
Let us come into his presence with thanksgiving;
　　let us make a joyful noise to him
　　　with songs of praise.　—Psalm 95:1,2

6

The Lord is in his holy temple;
　　let all the earth keep silence before him.

—Habakkuk 2:20

7

This is the day which the Lord has made;
　　let us rejoice and be glad in it.
O give thanks to the Lord for he is good;
　　for his steadfast love endures forever.

—Psalm 118:24,29

167

8

God is spirit, and those who worship him
must worship in spirit and truth.
. . . the true worshipers will worship the Father
in spirit and truth, for such the Father seeks
to worship him.   —John 4:24,23b

(To be read responsively by minister and congregation. The Choir may follow with response.)

1

(Congregation responses shown in italics)

O give thanks to the Lord, for he is good,
For his steadfast love endures for ever.
O give thanks to the God of gods,
For his steadfast love endures for ever.
O give thanks to the Lord of lords,
For his steadfast love endures for ever.
                —Psalm 136:1-3

2

O come, let us worship and bow down,
let us kneel before the Lord our Maker!
For he is our God,
and we are the people of his pasture,
and the sheep of his hand.
                —Psalm 95:6,7a

3

O sing to the Lord a new song;
sing to the Lord, all the earth
Sing to the Lord, bless his name;
tell of his salvation from day to day.
Declare his glory among the nations,
his marvelous works among all the peoples
For great is the Lord and greatly to be praised.
                —Psalm 96:1-4a

4

O come, let us sing to the Lord
let us make a joyful noise to the rock
of our salvation.
Let us come into his presence with thanksgiving,
let us make a joyful noise to him with songs of
praise.
For the Lord is a great God,
and a great King above all gods.
In his hand are the depths of the earth;
the heights of the mountains are his also.
The sea is his for he made it.
For his hands formed the dry land.

—Psalm 95:1-7

5

Bless the Lord O my soul, and
all that is within me, bless his holy name
Bless the Lord, O my soul,
and forget not all his benefits.

—Psalm 103:1,2

6

Praise the Lord, all nations!
Extol him, all peoples!
For great is his steadfast love toward us;
and the faithfulness of the Lord endures for ever.
Praise the Lord!

—Psalm 117

7

I will lift up my eyes to the hills.
From whence does my help come?
My help comes from the Lord who made heaven and earth.
He will not let your foot be moved, he who keeps you will
not slumber.
Behold, he who keeps Israel will neither slumber nor sleep.

—Psalm 121:1-4

O give thanks to the Lord, for He is good; for His steadfast love endures forever.

Let them thank the Lord for His steadfast love, for His wonderful works to the sons of men!

Let them extol Him in the congregation of the people, and praise Him in the assembly of the elders.

Whoever is wise, let him give heed to these things, let men consider the steadfast love of the Lord.

—Psalm 107:1,31,32,43

(Unison calls to worship)
Psalm 100 and 133

INVOCATIONS

1

With hearts overflowing with gladness we come again into Thy house, our Father. We are in these opening moments reminded of the many seasons of communion with Thee, and the good fellowship with one another granted us here. Be in our midst again today, we pray Thee, and quicken our spirits toward Thee, we pray, in the Master's name. Amen.

2

Our Father, and our God, we humbly come before Thee in these quiet moments, seeking to worship Thee, we trust, in spirit and in truth. Give us open minds, responsive hearts, that we may strengthen each other as our spirits drink deeply from the everlasting fountain of Thy love. Through Christ, our Lord, we pray. Amen.

3

O Lord, our hearts are filled with joy as we come again into this quiet sanctuary, where Thy people meet Thee. Do Thou just now shed abroad in our hearts Thy boundless love, and may we radiate toward those about us this great blessing which we feel today. Lift us above the everyday sins and sordidness of life, that our feet may be planted firmly on the Rock of Ages. We await the infilling of Thy Spirit. In Jesus name. Amen. —Paul S. Hayward

4

"Almighty God, of whom the whole family in heaven and on earth is named, we bless Thee for a fellowship which joins earth and heaven, and unites us with the worshiping faithful of ages past, who have found in Christ the true meaning of life. We bless Thee for a fellowship which at this moment of our awareness becomes world wide, and makes us one with men and women of every land and nation who know him as Saviour and Lord. May we be worthy members of this glorious company." —Alfred T. DeGroot

5

"O Lord, who makest the day to begin with the splendor of the sunrise, help us in this morning hour to lift our eyes on high, and to derive from the majesty of the pageant there unfolded a renewed sense of the dignity of human life, the joy of daily work. In His name Who is the Daybreak, we pray. Amen." —Alfred T. DeGroot

6

Heavenly Father, our hearts burn within us as once again we enter Thy sanctuary for worship. We are aware of the world-value of everyone about us, all of them Thy children, who share the abundance of Thy love. May this hour spent together in this house give richness to our thinking, clearness to our words, and guidance to our lives that we may take one step further toward that goal of perfection found in Thy Son Jesus Christ. In the name of Thy sinless Son, we pray. Amen.

7

O Holy Father, blessed be Thy name in all the earth. We come before Thee today with contrite hearts realizing our sinfulness, seeking and longing for Thy righteousness. Satisfy our souls today with manna from on high. Fill us with a sincere desire to do Thy will, for we ask it in the name of Christ, Thy fullest expression of love toward us. Humbly, we pray. Amen.

8

Our Father, as we enter into Thy house of prayer, and close behind us the doors to our earthly tasks, we would pray for a blessing, an infilling of Thy Spirit. Enlarge our vision, and show us the path of righteousness. We come in penitence, seeking to know what is good. In Christ's dear name, we pray. Amen.

9

"Almighty God, Who hast given us grace at this time with one accord to make our common supplications unto Thee; and dost promise that when two or three are gathered together in Thy name Thou wilt grant their requests; fulfill now, O Lord, the desires and petitions of Thy servants, as may be most expedient for them; granting us in this world knowledge of Thy truth, and in the world to come life everlasting. Amen."   —Chrysostom

10

"Our Father, again, as ever before, breathe upon us the blessings which we need—even that spirit of enlightenment, and of faith, and of love by which we shall know that we are Thy children, and rise into communion with Thee. Help us to lay aside all those influences that depress us, and which give strength to our senses. Give us those inspirations by which we may discern the invisible and the spiritual. And may the services of the sanctuary, and all the offerings of our hearts, our thoughts, and our fellowship, today, be acceptable to Thee. And, look lovingly upon us, that we may have joy and rejoicing in Thee. We ask it for Christ's sake. Amen."

—Henry Ward Beecher

SCRIPTURAL BENEDICTIONS

I Timothy 1:17

Philippians 4:7

Ephesians 3:20,21

II Corinthians 13:14

Psalm 67:1,2

Psalm 19:14

Numbers 6:24-26

Jude 1:24,25

Philippians 4:23

II Timothy 4:22

Philemon 1:25

Genesis 31:49b

GEMS FROM THE MINE OF EXPERIENCE
LET US PRAY

"Lord, make me an instrument of Thy peace.
Where there is hatred, let me sow love;
where there is injury, pardon;
where there is doubt, faith;
where there is despair, hope;
where there is darkness, light; and
where there is sadness, joy.

"O Divine Master, grant that I may not so much
        seek to be consoled as to console;
to be understood, as to understand;
to be loved, as to love;
for it is in giving that we receive;
it is in pardoning that we are pardoned;
and it is in dying that we are born to eternal life. Amen."

—St. Francis of Assisi

AFFIRMATION OF FAITH

LEADER: Where the Spirit of the Lord is, there is the one true Church, Apostolic and Universal, whose Holy Faith let us now reverently and sincerely declare:

LEADER AND PEOPLE:

We believe in the one God, Maker and Ruler of all things, Father of all men; the source of all goodness and beauty, all truth and love.

We believe in Jesus Christ, God manifest in the flesh, our Teacher, Example, and Redeemer, the Saviour of the world.

We believe in the Holy Spirit, God present with us for guidance, for comfort and for strength.

We believe in the forgiveness of sins, in the life of love and prayer, and in grace equal to every need.

We believe in the Word of God as the sufficient rule both of faith and of practice.

We believe in the Church as the fellowship for worship and for service of all who are united in the living Lord.

We believe in the kingdom of God as the divine rule of human society; and in the brotherhood of man under the Fatherhood of God.

We believe in the final triumph of righteousness, and in the life everlasting.

CHORAL AMEN

BORROWED

"He did not have a house where he could go
　　When it was night — when other men went
　　　　down
Small streets where children watched with eager
　　　　eyes,
　　Each one assured of shelter in the town.
The Christ sought refuge anywhere at all—
A house, an inn, the roadside, or a stall!

"He borrowed the boat in which He rode that day
　　He talked to throngs along the eastern lake;
It was a rented room to which He called
　　The chosen Twelve the night He bade them
　　　　break
The loaf with Him, and He rode, unafraid,
Another's colt in that triumph-parade.

"A man from Arimathaea had a tomb
　　Where Christ was placed when nails had done
　　　　their deed.
Not ever in the crowded days He knew
　　Did He have coins to satisfy a need.
They should not matter — these small things I crave,
Make me forget them, Father, and be brave!"

　　　　　　　　　　—Helen Welshimer

LIVING STONES

"On the Island of Jersey, in the English Channel, stands an old stone church. It has withstood the ravages of time, even though much of the cliff on which it was built has been worn away by the water and storms of the passing centuries. The walls of the church are made of stones of all sizes, for every member of the congregation contributed to them at least one stone, the best he could carry. The master builder used them all. There they are to this day. The rocks brought by the men have their place in the foundation. Stones large and small are there, and even pebbles that mothers had placed in the tiny hands of the babies.

"That old building stands as a symbol of what a church can be in a community—each worshiper and worker an essential living stone. We are needed, and the Master-Builder has a place for each of us. Whoever will may come—enriching the church by becoming an instrument for the grace of God."

—From *Secret Place*

WORLD-WIDE COMMUNION

He took the cup and gave thanks.
It was a cup of sorrow,
The agony of Gethsemane was in it;
The mockery of the crown of thorns was in it;
The thirst of Calvary was in it.
Yet He gave thanks.

It was the cup of death,
It held the symbol of his blood;
The shadow of the Cross was upon it,
Yet He took the cup and gave thanks.
And then, and then, He invited them to drink,
He gave thanks, for He had eyes to see;
Eyes that needed not the dim light of lamps,
Eyes that saw through the darkness and beyond.
He saw the cup as the cup of life,
The symbol of His power was in it;
The promise of forgiveness was in it,
The emblem of His love was in it.
He saw the cup as the cup of triumph—

The joy of the redeemed was in it,
The glory of His Crown was in it;
The vision of His Kingdom was in it;
And so He took the cup and gave thanks,
And invited them to drink.
It was the cup of their consecration.

—W. C. Smalley

A COMMUNION MEDITATION

This is the DAY most holy to the hungry soul,
 That from worldly cares would be freed;
This is the DAY most sacred to those who worship
 The Great Jehovah regardless of creed.
  This is the Lord's Day.

This is the HOUSE built by sacrificial gifts
 Of those who yearn for fellowship sweet;
This is the HOUSE, the sanctuary of the Holy,
 Where God has promised his saints to meet.
  This is the Lord's House.

This is the TABLE about which we gather,
 To commemorate the world's greatest sacrifice;
This is the TABLE bearing the memorial emblems
 Of Him who by His death paid the great price.
  This is the Lord's Table.
So, on this blessed LORD'S DAY let us come
 Into His HOUSE, the sanctuary of our God;
And from His TABLE, with contrite hearts,
 Eat and drink at the fountain of His Word;
  On the LORD'S DAY;
  In the LORD'S HOUSE;
  At the LORD'S TABLE.

—Oscar W. Riley

GOD'S CITIZEN

God's Citizen is thoughtful . . . He sees laws
Of love engraved upon the universe.
He studies God's commission to mankind.
Within both weak and strong he finds the gifts
Bequeathed by grace to soul and mind . . . He
    takes
To heart the great command, "Go forth, unlock
Earth's gifts and harness its stupendous force;
Be vital, valiant, kind . . . Awake to plain
Divine design! . . . Behold the laws revealed
In bold outline before our eyes!" . . . He prays.
He weighs Christ's Sermon On the Mount
    wherein
Love's fires flame high . . . and call each
    citizen
To dedicate his skills to God's great plan.
                    —Nell Rice Drake

BOOKS

Books are keys to wisdom's treasure,
Books are gates to lands of pleasure;
Books are paths that upward lead,
Books are friends. Come, let us read!
        —Emilie Poulson

FRIENDS

When others fail him, the wise man
                looks
To the sure companionship of
                books.
                    —Andrew Lang

FROM THE GATE OF THE YEAR

I said to the man who stood at the gate
of the year, "Give me light that I may
safely tread into the unknown," and he
replied, "Go out into the darkness and
put your hand into the hand of God.
That shall be to you better than light
and safer than any known way."

—M. Louise Haskins

IN THY PRESENCE

Lord, what a change within us one short hour
    Spent in Thy presence will avail to make;
    What heavy burdens from our bosoms take,
What parched grounds refresh as with a shower!
We kneel, and all around us seems to lower;
    We rise, and all, the distant and the near,
    Stands forth in sunny outline brave and clear;
We kneel, how weak; we rise how full of power!

—Richard C. Trench

A PRAYER FOR THE HOME

God's mercy spread the sheltering roof,
    Let faith make firm the floor;
May friend and stranger, all who come,
    Find love within the door.

May peace enfold each sleeping place,
    And health surround the board;
From all the lamps that light the halls,
    Be radiant joy outpoured.

Let kindness keep the hearth aglow,
    And through the windows shine;
Be Christlike living, on the walls,
    The pattern and design.

—T. L. Paine

STEWARDSHIP

"Now . . . concerning the collection"

"It is Sunday morning!

"We are sitting in our pews at . . . . Church. The deacons march down the aisle and turn again to pass among us. One stops at our pew. Hand after hand, the offering plate passes toward us.

"What. at this precise moment, is on our minds? What do we think as the plate is quietly passed?

"Do we regard these moments as an interruption of the real service . . . a necessary, yet slightly nettlesome formality to be dispatched as quickly as possible, then back to the 'real thing?' OR, do we see the offering plate as a visual symbol of our personal partnership in the affairs of Christ's Church?

"Giving is the ESSENCE of worship!

"The clue to the full meaning of the offering plate is in the Minister's words as he dispatches the Deacons on their rounds: 'Let us CONTINUE OUR WORSHIP with our tithes and offerings!'

"Giving, in fact, is the heart of worship. Just as the Cross itself is a symbol of Christ's supreme gift, so the offering plate becomes our symbol of worshipful giving. Next time the plate is passed, let us touch it reverently. Let us contribute to it prayerfully and pass it thoughtfully, realizing that at the moment it is in our hands we, of the entire congregation, are performing our own act of worship!

"Far from an interruption to the service, each of us enacts a private ceremony of penetrating significance."

THE KEY TO STEWARDSHIP
"First they gave themselves to the Lord."
—II Corinthians 8:5b

CHRISTIANITY

Christianity is a living spirit which should be cultivated until it becomes—

> As empirical as science
>
> As accurate as mathematics
>
> As practical as engineering
>
> As emotional as the drama
>
> As inspiring as art
>
> As aggressive as propaganda, and
>
> As irrepressible as an earthquake.

Christianity is the Spirit of Christ, alive to every test of every time.
—Chauncey R. Piety

GOD'S CALL TO YOUTH

God's call sounds through the centuries:
  Awake, O Youth, and know
Your total capabilities,
The waiting possibilities,
  What you should do, where you should go.

God's call rings through the universe:
  Advance, O Youth, today
Where things are bad and growing worse,
Where thinking straight is called a curse,
  Where tyrants hold the sway.

God calls you to make history:
  Advance, O Youth, and dare
Gethsemane and Calvary
To Light and lead humanity
  Where life gives life to share.

God calls to world community:
  Heed Him, O Youth, extend
His love, good will, and unity
And Kingdom's opportunity
  To every foe and friend.

—Chauncy R. Piety

FORM FOR THE ORDINATION OF MINISTERS*

The Relationship Between Minister and
Congregation

In the Apostolic Church there were Apostles, Prophets, Evangelists, Pastors, Teachers, Elders, Deacons, and Deaconesses, sometimes one person serving in several capacities. For Scriptural guidance in these matters read—

> I Peter 5:1
>
> II John 1
>
> III John 1
> Acts 6:5,8; 6:8,9; 8:5; 20:17
> Titus 1:5
> Philemon 2
> Colossians 4:15
>
> I Corinthians 16:19
> Ephesians 4:11,12

The term minister is the generally accepted and most universally used title of the person to whom the leadership of the church is given.

A candidate, having notified the Church of which he is a member, and the college in which he has qualified educationally, is presented for examination and ordination. The test should not be based primarily upon doctrinal, denominational tenets but rather upon the larger loyalty to the Scriptures with freedom of interpretation, his loyalty to the Church universal, and to the authority of Christ.

Those taking part in the ordination are ministers and elders of the Church. The principle of ordination reaches back to the Apostolic Church. The procedures afford opportunity for variation to match the local situation.

On the day appointed for the ordination, this order may be fitted into the Sunday morning or evening service of the church, or may be set up as a special order, whichever seems more appropriate. In any event, simplicity, dignity, beauty should prevail. The candidates should immediately precede the presiding minister in the procession, along with the other ministers and officers to the chancel, then the presiding minister may say:

We now come to the ordination of . . . .
to the office of Minister of the Gospel of Jesus Christ. Having diligently inquired into his fitness as required by the Scriptures in doctrine and manner of life, and especially the inner call of the Spirit, we present him before you to receive ordination with the Laying on of Hands, according to Apostolic example.

> (The presiding minister, turning to the candidate, who should arise, may read the following Scriptures beginning with—)

Hear the word of the Apostle Paul, found in Ephesians, the fourth chapter.

> (Read directly from the Bible)
> Ephesians 4:1-16
> Matthew 9:36-38
> John 10:1-16

CHARGE TO THE CANDIDATE: (By presiding minister or some other minister; then, the following questions are to be answered by the candidate.)

INQUIRY: Do you reaffirm your faith in Jesus Christ and your loyalty to Him as your Lord and Saviour, and will you strive to show forth His Spirit in all of your life and ministry?

> (Candidate answers—) "I do"

Do you affirm your belief in the Scriptures of the Old and New Testaments as containing the Word of God?

> (Answer—) "I do"

Do you affirm your determination in your study of the Scriptures, prayerfully in your attitude toward God, gentle, patient, and faithful in your ministrations to the people, friendly in your relations with other Christians and in your feelings and actions toward all races?

> (Answer—) "I will"

Do you affirm your determination to give your life to the ministry of Jesus Christ, whatever difficulties may lie in your way?

> (Answer—) "I will"

THE CONGREGATION'S EXPRESSION OF CONFIDENCE:

> (The presiding minister may then address the members of the church as follows:)

Do you affirm your confidence in................... and promise your prayers for God's blessing upon his ministry?

> (The people will then stand in giving the answer in the affirmative—afterwards be seated.)
>
> (The candidate shall then kneel, and the presiding minister and those officiating with him shall solemnly ordain him to the ministry by the laying on of hands and prayer, according to the Apostolic example. When they have placed their right hands on the candidate's head, the prayer of ordination may be given.)

PRAYER OF ORDINATION AND CONSECRATION

> (After the prayer, the ordained minister shall rise and the presiding minister, taking him by the right hand, shall say:)

We give you the right hand of fellowship to take part with us in the ministry of the Gospel of the Lord Jesus Christ.

> (Then let each of those assisting give the hand of fellowship to the newly ordained minister.)
>
> (It is often desirable to observe the Lord's Supper at this time.)

HYMN: "O Jesus I Have Promised"

BENEDICTION:

The grace of the Lord Jesus Christ and the love of God and the fellowship of the Holy Spirit be with you all. Amen.

—II Corinthians 13:14

*Adapted from *Christian Worship* by Peter Ainsley and H. C. Armstrong

185

CHARGE TO A NEWLY ORDAINED MINISTER

The Apostle Paul, who had much to say to young ministers, used a significant expression: "Remember Jesus Christ," II Timothy 2:8. May you ever remember Him whom you have confessed as your Lord and Saviour and who has called you to Himself and now sends you forth to be His minister.

REMEMBER, you belong to Him, you are not your own. "You have been bought with a price," therefore, make your ministry an offering to Him.

REMEMBER Jesus and His words, let them dwell in your heart that you may discover that truly He has the words of Eternal Life, and, that His words not only have the power to transform your life, but the lives of your hearers.

REMEMBER Jesus, who came "To seek and to save that which was lost and to give His life a ransom for the many." Make redemption and growth of persons your first objective in your ministry.

REMEMBER Jesus, "Who went about doing good, who came to minister, not to be ministered unto—." There is much good to be done in your lifetime, if you are willing to pay the price without being concerned over who gets the credit.

REMEMBER Jesus, who went to the Cross in complete surrender to God's will and who many times said, "He who would come after me, let him deny himself, take up his cross and follow me, for whosoever saveth his life shall lose it, but he that loses his life for my sake shall find it." There is no discipleship without a cross—and no Christian ministry!

REMEMBER Jesus, who had perfect faith in man even though he knew what was in man. He always looked upon people in terms of possibilities.

REMEMBER Jesus, who loved people, all kinds of people. He loved them because they were the children of His father. He came not to condemn them, but to love them. Therefore, before you can effectively preach the Gospel of Christ, you must have faith in people and love them devotedly.

REMEMBER Jesus, who "came preaching and teaching" and has commanded you to "go preach—teach." You are a man of the pulpit, a spokesman of God. Therefore, the pulpit for you becomes a distinctive symbol. Come to it often with a sense of urgency and never unprepared.

REMEMBER Jesus, who had perfect faith in God—as expressed through disciplined prayer and the study of the Bible. Your effectiveness will depend upon the way you draw upon these Divine resources.

REMEMBER Jesus, who "loved the church and gave Himself for it." It was He who said, "I will build my church." Make sure that the church belongs to Him and is dedicated to carrying out of His purpose and will. The church is the living visible body of Christ in the world today. Apart from this, the church has no right to exist, nothing to preach—it is merely "cumbering the ground."

REMEMBER, Jesus meets the needs of every human heart, therefore, bring the hearts of men to the heart of Christ.

REMEMBER Jesus and you will fulfill the purpose of your calling as a minister.
—Chester Crow

A SERVICE FOR THE INSTALLATION OF A
NEW MINISTER*

(This should be made a time of dedication for both pastor
and people. The leadership personnel for this service should
include both local and other ministers.)

PRELUDE: "Allegretto"............*Arr. from T. J. Haydn*

PROCESSIONAL HYMN: "God of Our Fathers, whose
Almighty Hand"
or
"Lead On, O King Eternal"
(The Congregation will rise as the processional begins.)

INVOCATION: (A visiting minister)

SCRIPTURE READING: II Timothy 2:1-7 (a visiting
minister)

SOLO: "The Lord Is My Light" (man)

SERMON: "The Measure of a Minister"—(some well-
known brotherhood leader)

DEDICATORY HYMN: "All Things Are Thine, No
Gift Have We"
"A Charge to Keep I Have"

COVENANT OF DEDICATION: (Led by Chairman of
Board of Elders)

LEADER: In the name of the Lord, Jesus Christ, the King and
Head of the Church, and in His presence, we are met
as a congregation to install as our minister, ...
.... Inasmuch as this solemn act in-
volves mutual obligations, I call upon you to unite
in a covenant of dedication. (Let the minister to be
installed stand, and make his declarations.)

MINISTER: Willingly do I affirm my ordination vows: Be-
lieving with all my heart that Jesus is the Christ, the

Son of the Living God, and accepting the Holy Scriptures as inspired of God through the Holy Spirit, it is my sincere desire to devote my life to the ministry of the Word; so to live as to bring credit and not dishonor to the Gospel which I preach; and to fulfill to my utmost ability, the office of a good minister of Jesus Christ. (The minister will be seated.)

LEADER: Will the Elders stand and make their declaration: Do you, severally and collectively, acknowledge the holy responsibilities of the office of the eldership to which you have been chosen. Do you affirm your love for this congregation, whose oversight you have; and do you offer yourself in a common service with your minister to tend the church of the Lord which He purchased with His own blood?

ELDERS (in unison): We do. (Elders will be seated.)

LEADER: Will the Deacons stand and make their declaration? Do you, severally and collectively, acknowledge the responsibilities of the office to which you have been chosen. Do you renew your pledge of loyalty to this church and the service to which you have been appointed. Do you promise to minister to all the material affairs of this congregation so as to maintain its reputation unsullied, and ever to keep it in good report by all those from without?

DEACONS: (in unison): We do. (Deacons will be seated.)

LEADER: Will the Choir stand and make their declaration? Do you covenant with God to ever dedicate your special gifts of music to His Church, to be His ministers of music in this congregation, and in cooperation with your minister to make this place a sanctuary of worship and a shrine of God's abiding presence?

CHOIR (in unison): We do. (Remain standing.)

LEADER: Will the congregation stand and make your declaration?

Do you affirm your membership in Christ's Church, and your fellowship in this congregation with those who have obtained a like precious faith, renewing your vows of fidelity to our Lord, Jesus Christ, and your allegiance to His Church. Do you solemnly covenant to work together with your minister to extend the Gospel in its purity and power in this community and throughout the world and, as faithful servants of the Lord, to give your pastor your utmost support in every way, according to your abilities and opportunities?

CONGREGATION (in unison): We do.

LEADER: Will the entire congregation please stand?

MINISTER: Brethren, standing with you, I affirm my willingness to be your minister; and now covenant with you that in the strength and grace of our Lord, Jesus Christ, I will live a holy and circumspect life among you, for an example; and will diligently and faithfully endeavor to perform all the duties of a good minister of Jesus Christ on behalf of this congregation, to the glory of His name and the edification of His Church.

INSTALLATION PRAYER: (Visiting minister)

LEADER: In the name of our Lord, Jesus Christ, the King and Head of the Church, we do hereby declare you . . . ., to be properly installed as the minister of this congregation of the . . . . Church, ... ; and we commend you to the grace of God in the discharge of all your duties as a minister of the Gospel. In token thereof, we give you the right hand of fellowship. The grace of our Lord, Jesus Christ, be with you. Amen.

Greetings from Leadership Personnel

HYMN OF CONSECRATION: "O Master, Let Me Walk
With Thee"
or
"O Jesus, I Have Promised"

BENEDICTION

POSTLUDE: A Medley of Great Hymns

*Adapted from *Christian Worship* by Peter Ainsley and H. C. Armstrong

A FORM FOR THE CONSECRATION OF CANDIDATES FOR THE MINISTRY AND THE MISSION FIELD

(Persons who have dedicated their lives to full-time Christian service, having been heard to speak on several occasions by the elders of the Church, and having been duly examined by a committee appointed by the Church Board, may be consecrated in a formal, yet simple, public service in the local church.)

OPENING SENTENCES: (Minister or Elder)

Praise is due Thee, O God in Zion;
and to Thee shall vows be performed . . .
Blessed is he whom Thou dost choose
and bring near,
to dwell in Thy courts
We shall be satisfied with the good—
of Thy house,
Thy holy temple.

—Psalm 65:1,4

"The harvest is plentiful, but the laborers are few; pray therefore the Lord of the harvest to send out laborers into his harvest.   —Matthew 9:37,38

PRAYER: (Minister or other Officer)

STATEMENT OF PURPOSE: (Minister)

Kind friends, we are instructed to pray for the increase of laborers in the harvest field of souls and in like manner to prove those who seek this position of leadership that no one may be consecrated hastily. This is a most sacred service and calls for those of good conduct and Christian integrity, able to speak or teach to lead others, and requires that we encourage them in preparing themselves by praying for them and lending full cooperation with them that they may become approved workmen, rightly handling the Word of Truth.

Therefore, being satisfied by personal observation and examination, the officers of the . . . .

192

Church are enthusiastically entering into this service of consecration, and announce their recognition of .... as candidate for the ministry (or missionary field).

MOMENTS OF AFFIRMATION: (The candidates, who have been seated at the front of the Church, will now stand before the minister as he calls for statements of affirmation.)

Do you reaffirm your faith in Christ and your love for His Church?

Do you believe the Scriptures of the Old and New Testaments to contain the Word of God?

Do you promise to study the Scriptures, laying them up in your heart, and do you promise to be diligent in prayer that you may grow in grace and in the knowledge of Christ?

Do you promise to be friendly in your attitude toward all Christians and all races?

Do you agree to continue your training and to enter into your chosen field of Christian service with the sincere devotion of your whole life?

(Having received an affirmative answer to each of these statements, the officers of the church will stand, then the minister shall say.)

For as much as you have made known to the Church the desire of your heart to serve God as a Christian minister (missionary) you are hereby consecrated and recognized for this exalted profession. The blessing of God be upon you, and the Spirit of Christ fill your heart.

PRAYER OF CONSECRATION

CLOSING HYMN

BENEDICTION

TEN COMMANDMENTS FOR AN ASSOCIATE MINISTRY

(From the crucible of experience)

1. One of the biggest jobs of an associate minister is to get the people to accept "you" without taking one iota from the "honor and glory and prestige" of the senior minister.

2. Work constantly to get the people to look forward to your call in its own right—and not simply as a substitute for the senior minister's call.

3. Accept the fact that you are an associate or assistant and yet not relegate yourself, mentally, into an inferior attitude. Work in your own right. You are not serving an apprenticeship.

4. Take all criticisms of the church or minister in strict confidence, even though it may not have been given in that way, and keep the senior minister aware of such criticism. He deserves to know.

5. Defend the minister at all costs. You must strive to unite the church, not divide it.

6. Be prepared for any emergency—
   Preach at the last moment.
   Any pastoral duty becomes yours if the senior minister becomes incapacitated.

7. Always give the senior minister first chance to make certain calls. He is the shepherd of the flock. Be sure he knows of events he may not be aware of—tragedy, death, etc.

8. Inform the senior minister immediately of any serious illness you discover which he may not be aware of. He, through his own knowledge, or from you, should know everything about the people at all times.

9. Try to compliment the senior minister at all times. I do not mean, say nice things about him, but I mean: he is human, and yet must be all things to all people. There are some places he might be weak; strive to help him by making yourself stronger at these points of weakness.

10. Remember, you are not only serving a congregation, YOU ARE SERVING THE MASTER, and you are serving another minister.

—Don J. VerDuin.

NOTE: Offered here for the guidance of those who may be called to serve in this significant position.

AN INSTALLATION SERVICE FOR CHRISTIAN WOMEN'S FELLOWSHIP

INTRODUCTORY STATEMENT

God confronted Moses at the burning bush with the command, "put off your shoes from your feet, for the place on which you are standing is holy ground." In this spirit we approach this installation service with reverence and in prayer. This is the place, and this is the moment of high dedication.

God is confronting these women with a task . . . a task which will take them where they have never ventured before; which will engage them in duties they have never before dared to attempt. This will demand of them good judgment and much labor. Often they will be surrounded with discouragement, then again they will break forth in great joy at the achievements in which they will share.

God is confronting us with ventures of faith and of action as yet unattained. This is a moment of high and holy purpose. Let us not enter into it lightly . . . but rather in deep earnestness, realizing that God is in our midst.

The purpose of the Christian Women's Fellowship is to develop all women in Christian living and Christian service, that they may grow in spirit, intellect and in service to follow more and more closely the footsteps of the Master. He "went about doing good." We dare not fail Him in the supreme enterprise of bringing in the Kingdom.

Feeling the presence of God in our midst we humbly confess our unworthiness. When we see His righteousness and love, His justice and mercy, we become more and more conscious of our own imperfections. Let us pray in silence, but with open hearts, holding no secrets but confessing all to our Maker and Redeemer . . . seeking His pardon, asking in penitence His forgiveness.

(silence)

Hear these our earnest prayers, O God, for in His holy name we pray. Amen.

A WORD OF APPRECIATION

To outgoing officers who have served faithfully through the year just closing, we offer a sincere word of commendation for a job well done. This expression comes from all the women of our churches. How better could our love for you be expressed than in words of Paul, to the Thessalonians—

"We give thanks to God always for you all, constantly mentioning you in our prayers, remembering before our God and Father your work of faith and labor of love and steadfastness of hope in our Lord Jesus Christ."—I Thessalonians 1:2,3

INCOMING OFFICERS

Will the incoming officers please come forward?

To you, officers-elect of the Christian Women's Fellowship for the coming year—I charge you to remember that Christ called Zaccheus in these words—

"Make haste and come down for I must stay at your house today."

So Jesus calls you to prepare to receive, not only an office, but also your Master and Saviour. Without Him you can do nothing.

TO THE ASSEMBLED GROUP:

To this congregation of women, I say: "These are called to lead in a fellowship of Christian women. Make certain that the fellowship is not diminished in effectiveness through your absence or lack of interest. Make it a strong, vigorous fellowship by your contribution and sustained richness of personality through God's grace.

Again in the words of Paul:

"We beseech you, brethren, to respect those who labor among you and are over you in the Lord and admonish you, and to esteem them very highly in love because of their work . . . and we exhort you, brethren, admonish the idle, encourage the fainthearted, help the weak, be patient with them all . . . Rejoice always, pray constantly, give thanks in all circumstances; for this is the will of God in Christ Jesus for you."

—I Thessalonians 4:12-18

To the President:

You have been chosen as president of the Christian Women's Fellowship because of your leadership qualities, because of your deep consecration, and your dependability to see a job through. You will be expected to manifest enthusiasm, vision, courage, faithfulness and to show a willing spirit. May the CWF, wherever you see the emblem, remind you of the local, district, state and world-wide fellowship of Christian women as together we follow the Cross of Christ.

To the Vice-President:

As first Vice-President in charge of co-ordinating the program of the CWF, the symbol of your office would be that of a circle. Yours is the responsibility of binding this group together in a program of real Christian effectiveness. May the circle ever expand under your guidance until it includes all who have chosen the Lord, Jesus Christ.

To the Secretary:

In your office as secretary for the CWF you have a very meaningful position. The emblem of the CWF will hold significant meaning through the records you will keep with diligence and accuracy. Yours will be the job of recording progress.

To the Treasurer:

In serving as treasurer your work will give the "F" of the emblem—CWF—additional significance as you receive, record and disburse funds of this Christian enterprise. Every worthwhile project must have financial undergirding. Financing the work is a sacred trust in Christian stewardship.

To the Worship Director:

The dominant meaning of the CWF emblem resides in the Cross. It is through this symbol that we must view all of life. Your responsibility as worship chairman will be to hold high the Cross, and to guide the spirit of consecration and devotion into radiant spiritual fields of fruitfulness in Christ.

To the Study Director:

As chairman of Study you will recognize in the term "Women" a symbol of growing and developing personality. It will be your responsibility to challenge all of the women to study that they may "show themselves approved unto God," informed, enlightened Christians.

To the Service Director:

As Service Director in charge of Service Projects the term "Women" in the CWF symbolizes a vibrant, growing personality. It will be your task to channel the energy, eagerness and desire to be useful unto necessary tasks to meet real needs.

Solo: "A Charge to Keep I Have"

Closing Prayer of Consecration:

> (This may be developed in the form of a Litany of Consecration if desired.)

INSTALLATION SERVICE FOR CHRISTIAN MEN'S FELLOWSHIP OFFICERS*

HYMN: "Jesus Calls Us" (stanzas 1, 2, 4)

PRAYER

THE OFFICERS PLEDGE:

"I do solemnly pledge, by the help of Almighty God, and through the inspiration that comes from our Lord, Jesus Christ, that I will endeavor to serve the Christian Men's Fellowship of .... Church to the best of my ability, for the year ...... I will endeavor to attend the regular services of the Church, to lead in the program of evangelism of the Church, and to cultivate the minds of the manhood of the Church, so that they might wisely understand the whole program of the Church. This I will do, so help me God, in the due performance of the same."

THE MEMBERS PLEDGE:

"We, the members of the Christian Men's Fellowship of .... Church, have of our own choice elected for the year the officers now being installed. We sincerely and truly realize that these officers cannot perform their sacred task without the unanimous and harmonious support of each of us. We, therefore, pledge our allegiance to their leadership, and by the help of Almighty God and our Blessed Saviour, we will endeavor to give to them our loyal support during the year ...."

OFFICERS AND MEMBERS REPEAT THE COVENANT:

"I covenant with God:

1. To be present at the Communion Table and regular Church services and to endeavor to induce other members to do likewise.

2. To recruit men for Christ by winning them through personal contact and invitation to attend Church.

3. To support the work of the Church at home and to the uttermost parts of the world.

CONSECRATION PRAYER: (Incoming President)

RESPONSE: "Have Thine Own Way" (stanzas 1 and 4)

BENEDICTION

*Compiled by Nimmo Goldston,

CHAPTER VI

THE MINISTER KEEPS A RECORD OF SERVICES

200

RECORD OF MARRIAGES

Date	Names	Places and Witnesses
2/25/96	Kristal Brown to Marcus Stacy	Nicholasville, KY. Jonathan K. Brown & Gwen Stidham-Neff
7/05/97	William T. Fields to Kimberly Millen	Big Waland Beverly Baker & Melissa Hunt

RECORD

RECORD OF MARRIAGES

Date	Names	Places and Witnesses

RECORD

RECORD OF MARRIAGES

Date	Names	Places and Witnesses

RECORD

RECORD OF FUNERALS

Date	Name	Age	Place
/ 1388	Joshua Strong Maggard F.H.	91	HAZARD, KY
Aug 24, 89	PEARL GARRIS	71	DWARF BABTIS
MOY 91	LYNN PINSON	48	LEXINGTON, KY
Aug 92	GETEN PINSON	78	BYESVILLE, C
Aug 19, 95	MARY BAKER	70	Big CREEK E
Mar. 11, 99	Marie Bard	79	Breashear F.4
Jan 11, 99	HERSHEL DIXON	79	EAGLE F.H.
FEB 2001	Velria Baby	62	Byesville, Oh.
Sept 7, 2005	CORA PINSON	86	BYESVILLE, Oh
DEC 20, 05	RAYMOND BAILEY		BYESVILLE, Ohio

204

RECORD

RECORD OF FUNERALS

Date	Name	Age	Place

RECORD

RECORD OF FUNERALS

Date	Name	Age	Place

RECORD

RECORD OF SPECIAL OCCASIONS

Date	Event	Place and Other Data

RECORD

RECORD OF SPECIAL OCCASIONS

Date	Event	Place and Other Data

RECORD

RECORD OF SPECIAL OCCASIONS

Date	Event	Place and Other Data

RECORD

Date	Name of Candidate	Name and Location of Church

RECORD

RECORD OF BAPTISMS

Date	Name of Candidate	Name and Location of Church

RECORD

RECORD OF BAPTISMS

Date	Name of Candidate	Name and Location of Church

RECORD

THE MINISTER'S TIMOTHIES*

Date	Name of Timothy	Name and Location of Church

*Some churches place a picture of each young person who has entered full-time religious work in the church's narthex gallery.

RECORD

CONVENTIONS ATTENDED

Date	Name of the Convention	Convention Location

RECORD

CONVENTIONS ATTENDED

Date	Name of the Convention	Convention Location

RECORD

CONVENTIONS ATTENDED

Date	Name of the Convention	Convention Location

RECORD

Date	Name of the Convention	Convention Location

RECORD

Through an Adequate Filing System*

In all probability there are as many filing systems as there are ministers, provided every minister has a system. The type of ministry in which one is engaged will determine the system.

When it comes to a minister's library the need may call for the Dewey Decimal System, which would follow this procedure:

000-099	General
100-199	Philosophy, Psychology, Ethics
200-299	Religion
300-399	Sociology, Government, Economics, Law, Education
400-499	Languages
500-599	Science, Mathematics, Astronomy, Geology, Biology, Physics
600-699	Useful Arts—Medicine, Engineering, Home Economics
700-799	Fine Arts, Architecture, Needlework, Printing, Music, Drama, Amusements
800-899	Literature
900-999	History, Travel, Biography

Usually a minister will follow a simpler plan, arranging his books by authors alphabetically, giving the initial letter of the surname of the author to each book, then numbering each book under each letter, eg., A-1, A-2. Later books may be numbered, eg., A-1a, A-2a. By identifying each book in this way the library will be quite usable. Then a card record may be made of each book and the cards filed under subjects, eg., Worship, Administration, Committees, Psychology, Sermons, etc.

*Baker Book House, Grand Rapids, Michigan, offers a system that takes into account every conceivable want on the part of the minister seeking a filing system. When once set up, this system will make books, clippings, sermon notes and other valuable material in the minister's study readily accessible.

CALENDAR
A Table to Find Easter Day from

1956 to 2012 A. D.

*The years marked with an asterisk are Leap Years.

1956*	...April 1	1985	...April 7
1957	...April 21	1986	...Mar 30
1958	...April 6	1987	...April 19
1959	...Mar 29	1988*	...April 3
1960*	...April 17	1989	...Mar 26
1961	...April 2	1990	...April 15
1962	...April 22	1991	...Mar 31
1963	...April 14	1992*	...April 19
1964*	...Mar 29	1993	...April 11
1965	...April 18	1994	...April 3
1966	...April 10	1995	...April 16
1967	...Mar 26	1996*	...April 7
1968*	...April 14	1997	...Mar 30
1969	...April 6	1998	...April 12
1970	...Mar 29	1999	...April 4
1971	...April 11	2000*	...April 23
1972*	...April 2	2001	...April 15
1973	...April 22	2002	...Mar 31
1974	...April 14	2003	...April 20
1975	...Mar 30	2004*	...April 11
1976*	...April 18	2005	...Mar 27
1977	...April 10	2006	...April 16
1978	...Mar 26	2007	...April 8
1979	...April 15	2008*	...Mar 23
1980*	...April 6	2009	...April 12
1981	...April 19	2010	...April 4
1982	...April 11	2011	...April 24
1983	...April 3	2012*	...April 8
1984*	...April 22		

SUGGESTED PREACHING BUDGET FOR THE CHRISTIAN YEAR

Literature is available each year from the headquarters of your Communion outlining in complete detail the Christian Year with the various emphases to guide ministers and local churches in building an adequate program of work for the local church. As ministers, we will do well to give due consideration to this literature, not to follow it with slavish exactness and dead routine, but to use it as a channel of Christian growth and service.

Would it not be wise for the minister to choose his sermon subjects for the whole year, in keeping with current emphases, then arrange his file of illustrations and other preaching material, building in helpful items as the Sundays move along? Yes, you may change a sermon subject here and there through the year as you make current adjustment, but a sermon budget for the year will prove exceedingly helpful if given a fair and unprejudiced trial. The minister who plans his pulpit messages well in advance will find great joy and satisfaction for himself and for his congregation in this practice. Here is the Christian Year in brief—

THE CHRISTIAN YEAR
(Following the calendar year for convenience)

JANUARY
NEW YEAR SUNDAY—Sunday before New Year's Day.

WEEK OF PRAYER—First full week in January.

EPIPHANY—January 6, Visit of the Magi.

CHURCH AND ECONOMIC LIFE WEEK—Third Week in January.

FEBRUARY
YOUTH SUNDAY—Beginning of Youth Week, Boy Scout Week.

RACE RELATIONS SUNDAY—Sunday nearest February 12.

BROTHERHOOD DAY—Sunday nearest February 22.

WEEK OF COMPASSION—Begins with Brotherhood Sunday.

MARCH AND APRIL
WORLD MISSION DAY—First Sunday in March.

ASH WEDNESDAY—Beginning of Lent, seventh week before Easter.

WORLD DAY OF PRAYER FOR WOMEN—First Friday in Lent, six weeks before Good Friday.

PALM SUNDAY—The Sunday before Easter.

HOLY WEEK—Week between Palm Sunday and Easter.

MAUNDY THURSDAY—Inauguration of the Lord's Supper.

GOOD FRIDAY—The Day of Crucifixion.

EASTER—Commemorating the Resurrection.

EASTER TO PENTECOST—Period of Stewardship Emphasis.

CHRISTIAN HIGHER EDUCATION—Christian Education, usually the second Sunday after Easter.

PENTECOST—Christian Unity, seventh Sunday after Easter.

MAY
NATIONAL (Christian) FAMILY WEEK—First full week in May.

MAY FELLOWSHIP DAY FOR WOMEN—First Friday in May.

FESTIVAL OF THE CHRISTIAN HOME—Second Sunday in May, Mother's Day.

RURAL LIFE SUNDAY—Fifth Sunday after Easter.

MEMORIAL SUNDAY—Sunday nearest May 30.

CHRISTIAN UNITY SUNDAY—(See Pentecost).

JUNE
CHILDREN'S DAY—First Sunday in June, World Missions.

ACHIEVEMENT DAY—For review of the year, third Sunday.

FATHER'S DAY—Third Sunday.

NATURE SUNDAY—Fourth Sunday.

JULY

INDEPENDENCE SUNDAY—Sunday before July 4.

AUGUST

FESTIVAL OF CHRIST THE KING—Second Sunday before Labor Day.

SEPTEMBER

LABOR SUNDAY—The Sunday before the first Monday.

GO TO COLLEGE SUNDAY—AND RECOGNITION OF THE OPENING OF THE PUBLIC SCHOOLS—Second Sunday.

RALLY DAY—Third or fourth Sunday.

CHURCH PROGRAM PLANNING AND RELIGIOUS EDUCATION WEEK—Last full week of September.

OCTOBER

WORLD COMMUNION SUNDAY—First Sunday.

CHURCH LOYALTY SEASON—Six weeks following World Communion Sunday.

SUNDAY OF THE MINISTRY—Second Sunday.

LAYMEN'S SUNDAY—Third Sunday.

WORLD ORDER SUNDAY—Sunday before October 2, the anniversary of the United Nations Charter.

REFORMATION SUNDAY—Recognizing the beginning of Protestantism, last Sunday.

CHRISTIAN LITERATURE WEEK—Last week in October or first week in November.

NOVEMBER

WOMEN'S WORLD COMMUNITY DAY—First Friday.

MEN AND MISSIONS DAY—Second Sunday.

THANKSGIVING SUNDAY—Sunday before Thanksgiving.

THANKSGIVING DAY—Fourth Thursday.

ADVENT SUNDAY—Fourth Sunday before Christmas, and beginning of the Liturgical Year Calendar.

DECEMBER

WOMEN'S DAY—First Sunday, World Missions.

UNIVERSAL BIBLE SUNDAY—Second Sunday.

CHRISTMAS SUNDAY—Sunday before Christmas.

STUDENT RECOGNITION SUNDAY—Some Sunday during the Christmas holidays.

INDEX OF POEMS

(By Authors)

223

A CONDENSED ALPHABETICAL INDEX